new connections
in chain mail jewelry with
rubber and glass rings

KAT WISNIEWSKI

KALMBACH BOOKS

Waukesha, Wisconsin

Dedication:
To my brother, Adam.

Kalmbach Books
21027 Crossroads Circle
Waukesha, Wisconsin 53186
www.JewelryAndBeadingStore.com

© 2016 Kat Wisniewski

All projects in this book appear royalty-free. That is, all projects in *New Connections in Chain Mail Jewelry with Rubber and Glass Rings* are available to individual consumers for reproduction. The designer, Kat Wisniewski, encourages you to make these beautiful pieces of jewelry to share with others or sell for profit if you so wish.

Published in 2016
20 19 18 17 16 15   1 2 3 4 5

Manufactured in China

ISBN: 978-1-62700-237-0
EISBN: 978-1-62700-238-7

Editor: Erica Swanson
Book Design: Lisa Schroeder
Photographer: William Zuback

Library of Congress Control Number: 2015941331

contents

Introduction 4

BASICS

How to Use This Book 6

Materials and Components 8

Tools 10

Techniques... 13

PROJECTS

Looped Earrings.................................... 18

Looped Drop Earrings 20

Decadent Confection Bracelet................ 22

Synthesis Necklace............................... 25

Oracle Pendant 29

Ninja Star Earrings 32

Arched Ascent Bracelet 35

Parallel Bars Bracelet........................... 39

To the Point Earrings............................ 43

Celtic Crossroads Bracelet 46

Caterpillar Earrings............................... 50

Japanese Rubber Bloom Earrings........... 54

Buoyant Promenade Necklace................ 58

Fold & Gather Linear Star Pendant 62

Celtic Diamond Pendant 66

Crosscut Bracelet 70

Interwoven Network Bracelet 74

Encapsulated Delicacy Bracelet............. 78

Into Orbit Necklace............................... 81

Arctic Sphere Bracelet.......................... 85

Lock & Twist Bracelet 89

Lock & Twist Pendant............................ 93

Lustrous Stitched Bracelet 97

Space Oddity Pendant 101

Interstellar Pendant.............................. 105

Glossary.. 109

Acknowledgments and About the Author........... 111

introduction

When I decided to write this book, I thought about how to present my favorite craft as approachable, fun, and modern, with a hint of elegance. My specialty is in creating glass and rubber chain mail designs, with bold colors and chic style. I felt strongly that my creative spark would be appreciated by other crafty types, too. I knew there wasn't a vast amount of tutorials that used glass rings and only a handful of rubber chain mail tutorials, so with my years of chain mail tutorial writing and publishing experience, I knew I was the perfect person for the job.

Students have many times asked, "How did you come up with that?" I typically answer by saying, "Well, I have lots and lots of patience." I sit for hours and hours, trying various combinations of ring sizes, glass rings, and rubber rings until I come up with original designs or an updated version of older favorites. Sure, I have plenty of failed experiments, but so many amazing patterns have come about from trial and error—and, of course, patience. I usually start with a favorite ring size, figure out what can go in it or around it in a new way, and then keep playing from there. I want to inspire you to create not just the projects in this book, but to come up with fresh ideas from everything you learn!

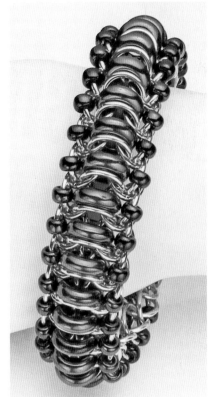

This book is geared toward beginners with each project presented in order of difficulty, starting with the easiest. A more advanced chain mailer can pick up this book and definitely be challenged and even learn a new skill in combining glass and rubber into their designs. You may notice this is not an all-inclusive, everything-there-is-to-possibily-know-about-chain mail book. There are a great variety of books available that have gone into great detail about various topics. *New Connections* is mainly project based, with some basic information to get you going. I want you to take this creative journey with me and feel the joy of completing each project, moving on to tackle the next one and increasing your skill level as you progress through the book. All the projects have fun, shiny colors and details about what tools to use are included throughout each project.

Oh and guess what? You can make AND sell anything that you make from this book! My gift is teaching, and I am happy to share my designs and patterns to help my fellow artists make a bit of money from this lovely craft.

What you'll see in this book:
- Innovative glass and rubber designs using aluminum and anodized aluminum as the primary metals.
- What are the available types of pliers? Which pliers to use for what ring sizes and for which projects?
- How to troubleshoot what ring sizes will work with the glass and rubber pieces.
- A quick discussion about wire gauges, inner diameter, aspect ratio and a few other technical terms.
- How to properly open and close jump rings for the most professional results.
- More goodies to be revealed!

I want to **inspire** you to create not just the projects in this book, but to come up with **fresh ideas** from everything you **learn!**

basics
HOW TO USE THIS BOOK

Glossary
There are many terms you may want to become familiar with before diving in to this book. Give the glossary a quick look and review all of the jump ring jargon.

Project organization
The projects are organized in order of the most simple to the more complex and time intensive. I had beginners in mind when creating each project; however as beginners progress through each project, they will learn skills and techniques that will help them accomplish even the most difficult of weaves. The projects near the end of the book are more challenging due to the tightness of the weaves, the amount of rings needed, and/or the time commitment required to finish them.

Each project will list the approximate time frame it will take to complete it. I've developed these time frames based on the time it takes an average student to complete a similar project if making it for the first time.

Supplies
There is a supply chart at the start of each project that includes ring sizes, ring counts, findings, and basic tools. All of the metal, glass, and rubber rings, as well as beads and other components, are listed by the common supplier name or measurement. So if a glass ring is listed as 14mm, that is how the vendor refers to it, even though its actual measurement is slightly different (because many suppliers tend to round up the numbers). Metal rings are listed by their mandrel size, with its closest millimeter size in parentheses. Most suppliers sell jump rings by listing the mandrel size and not the actual finished measured size. The actual measured size of that ring will be different when coiling, springback, and the anodizing process (which can slightly strip the ring's thickness away) are taken into account. The gauge of the wire is listed by the gauge number with the millimeter convesion of the wire thickness directly after it. The millimeter conversion may be needed to make sure the rings from your supplier match the measurements used in the book.

The supply list will also include the actual measured aspect ratio (AR) for each of the rings used (see aspect ratio discussion on p. 10). Beginners need not be too concerned with the AR numbers, but I've included them for those who are curious.

Here's a quick example of the difference between the supplier listing and the actual measurements. A ring size is listed as ¼" ID (6.4mm) 18 gauge (1.2mm). So this means the mandrel used was ¼", which converts to approximately 6.4mm. The wire used was 18-gauge, which measures approximately 1.2mm. I know from using my calipers to measure that the ring actually measures about 6.8mm ID and has a wire diameter closer to 1.0. The listed mandrel size measurements are always different than the actual measurements. All of the projects in this book have been thoroughly tested and work with the exact listed metals and ring sizes.

Materials for all of the projects in this book may be found at your local bead store or through online suppliers. If you have trouble locating any specific materials, please visit the book's website at www.newconnectionsbook.com. In addition to potential suppliers, you will find bonus tips, tool information, and kits for each project supplied by Mhai o Mhai Beads!

Ring substitutions

Any project that lists "anodized aluminum" can be substituted with plain aluminum (or bright aluminum). If it lists "aluminum," you can choose to use "anodized aluminum" instead. Many of the projects can made with copper, brass, bronze, and steel in the same ring sizes, but you must check with your supplier to make sure the sizes match. All of the projects are done with Standard Wire Gauge (SWG) ring sizes (see SWG discussion on p. 9).

Glass ring thicknesses and hole sizes

The glass rings are shiny and beautiful in the designs, but they can sometimes be difficult to work with. If you order from a single supplier, each batch is fairly consistent; however, sometimes there are dye lot issues or problems with the thickness of the rings. Some suppliers have thick glass rings and others have thin glass rings, which means the hole sizes and the outer diameters will be slightly different also.

The thin glass rings tend not to work as well for tighter weaves. Sometimes the thicker glass rings are just a bit too thick and then the jump ring sizes have to be adjusted in the hopes of finding something that works. There are occasions when a particular weave has worked with particular glass rings in the past and then suddenly it won't work any longer. This happens because of slight changes to the thickness in the glass rings and also due to very slight metal ring size changes from the supplier.

Keep in mind, jump ring sizes may have to adjust to accommodate changes in the glass rings. The projects will list which types of glass rings can be used. You can assume if a size is not listed, then it will not work well for that weave with the accompanying ring sizes. The suppliers of glass rings tend to round up from the actual measured outer and inner diameters. For example, the large glass rings are listed everywhere online as 14mm. They are referring to the outer diameter (OD) only. The actual measured OD is 13.7mm. Why does this matter? The 0.3mm difference can affect if a weave will work or not, but I've already made sure that all the patterns in this book will work with the listed sizes. Any exceptions will be noted.

Are you left-handed?

I've been teaching left-hand students for many years, and normally I'd have a separate left-handed version of the tutorial just for you. I could not include a left-handed version of each project, so please bear with the right-handed people. You can place a mirror in front of the book so that the photos appear from the left-side orientation. When opening your rings, it's a great idea to pull the left side of the ring toward you so that you can weave more comfortably by picking up the ring from the left side that is sticking up from your work surface.

9.5mm OD x3.5mm glass rings

9mm OD glass rings

14mm OD glass rings

MATERIALS & COMPONENTS

I've limited the materials to help make it easier to source the rings from just a few suppliers. Of course there are many other metals and materials you could use to make chain mail, and certainly you can make your own rings. Please take notice of the measurements listed per project. Some weaves need exact measurements and specific materials for them to work properly. When exceptions can be made, I will note them within each project.

Czech pressed glass rings
The glass rings are machine made, so they are fairly consistent. These glass rings are known by a variety of names: donut beads, cheerio beads, fisher rings, and glass donut rings. They are available in various colors.

Glass beads
I use 6º Miyuki seed beads and 3º Toho seed beads in this book. These particular brands have the most consistent sizing with generous holes. Czech and other seed beads may have smaller holes and inconsistent sizing. Note that pearlized, painted, Duracoat or other added finishes may come off.

Steel donut rings
Made out of stainless steel, these are quite consistent in shape and hole size. They are a bit weighty though, so you don't want to use too many in a single piece of jewelry.

Silicone rubber rings
Silicone is soft and flexible and tends to be available in brighter colors. Rubber rings are made from molds that allow for consistency in size from ring to ring.

Aluminum rings
This is a semi-soft metal that has a fair amount of springback. The springback adds to its strength, making this a very durable metal. It is a great choice for beginners due to its low cost. Aluminum cannot be work-hardened, as overworking the metal makes it brittle.

Anodized aluminum rings
This is aluminum that has gone through a dye process to achieve a wide variety of colors. It is fairly low-cost and great for beginners. As there is a dye-coating on these rings, you'll need to be very gentle with the tips of the pliers while working the rings.

Enameled copper rings
These rings are not truly enameled. They are made of a soft copper that is coated in thin plastic coloring. Enameled copper is quite soft, yet the plastic coloring is quite durable. Enameled copper is so soft it is quite easy to bend and twist the ring out of shape.

Stainless steel rings
This is one of the strongest chain mail metals available. It has a strong temper with a lot of springback. There is also a slightly softer annealed steel available, which makes it easier to work with. 16-gauge and even some 18-gauge steel can be challenging to work with.

Bronze rings
Bronze is also a very strong metal that weighs slightly more than stainless steel. It is a copper alloy that has more of a golden brown tone, whereas copper has more of a reddish tone. Bronze has a firm temper and a good amount of springback. Strong hands are needed for thicker gauges.

FINDINGS

I almost exclusively use the following findings because of their strength, durability, and ease to clean.

There are many other available materials that are not used in this book, yet are widely available, such as copper, jewelry brass, galvanized steel, niobium, sterling, gold-filled, and more. Different metals have different measurements that must be accounted for when substituting them for any of the projects in this book.

Rhodium-plated, matte black, or stainless steel lobster claw clasps
These match pre-made chain and jump rings nearly perfectly. They do not tarnish or yellow over time like plated items do. The swivel is fantastic because it will move with your movement and minimize kinks and twisting of the chains.

Toggle clasps
I prefer Tierra Cast toggles overall for their superior finishes and beautiful designs. I especially like the rhodium-plated products, which match aluminum products so well. It's good to have basic large toggles on hand that complement any design.

Earring wires
For aluminum or steel, I use surgical steel earring wires. I also keep plain niobium earring wires on hand for those who might be extra sensitive to metals. For anything with a darker color or black, I use anodized niobium black earring wires.

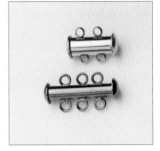

Multi-strand slide clasp
I enjoy the steel multi-strand clasp, as it does not tarnish or rust. (The steel ones are hard to find, so you can use silver-plate instead.) The gunmetal finish works well with the iridescent gunmetal or black color rings.

JUMP RINGS

Ring properties and jump ring jargon
Let's quickly discuss saw-cut versus machine-cut jump rings. Saw-cut jump rings have been cut with a precise and thin blade, where only a small piece of metal (also called the kerf, which is the thickness of the blade) is missing. Machine-cut jump rings are created when a machine cuts down into the coil, leaving a slight divit or triangle cut on the ring. Some people use wire cutters, which also creates a slight pinch of the metal at the ends of each ring. When closing a saw-cut ring, the cut is precisely flush and should line up seamlessly. When closing a saw-cut ring, the ends are almost flush and you will notice a small piece of metal missing and possibly a rough feel. The photos show two closed rings. The black one is the machine-cut ring and the aluminum one is the saw-cut ring. I only use saw-cut jump rings in this book.

Wire is available in two measurement systems:
AWG: American Wire Gauge, also known as Brown & Sharpe (thinner) is used for precious metals like sterling, gold, and niobium.

SWG: Standard Wire Gauge, also known as British Imperial Standard (thicker) is used for base metals such as aluminum, anodized aluminum, copper, steel, bronze, brass, and more. Copper and jewelry brass can be found in both systems. This book uses SWG gauges.

Wire Gauge	SWG- Base metals (thicker)	AWG- Precious Metals (thinner)
24	0.56mm	0.51mm
22	0.71mm	0.64mm
21	—	0.72mm
20	0.81mm*	0.81mm*
19	1.0mm	0.91mm
18	1.22mm	1.02mm
17	—	1.15mm
16	1.63mm	1.29mm
15	—	1.45mm
14	2.03mm	1.63mm
13	—	1.83mm
12	2.64mm	2.05mm

*The 20-gauge used for these projects measures about 0.8mm, although some online wire suppliers list 20-gauge SWG as being 0.9mm.

More about SWG

The measurement (given in millimeters) must be nearly the same per system to ensure the best option when converting a project from base metal to precious metal and the inverse. Notice in the chart that 80-gauge SWG (1.22mm) is closest in millimeter measurements to 17-gauge AWG (1.5mm). 17-gauge AWG (ex. sterling) can be used as a substittue for 18-gauge SWG (ex. aluminum).

Some weaves will not work in the same wire gauge number in both SWG and AWG. 18-gauge SWG is 1.2mm and in AWG, it measures 1.024mm. 1.024mm is thinner than 1.2mm thickness.

Inner diameter

Rings can be made either on inch mandrels or millimeter mandrels, which affects the size of the inner diameter (ID) of the ring. The finished jump ring size is usually larger than the mandrel on which the wire was wrapped (aka coiled). This is because the wire unwinds, resists, and springs back a bit as it leaves the mandrel. Steel, which is has a very strong temper, has more springback than copper, which is very soft. Also, remember the actual measured inner diameter is larger than the mandrel the wire was wound on.

Chain mail suppliers sell jump rings either in inch sizes, such as 5/32" or in millimeter sizes, such as 4.5mm. This means that the wire was wound either on inch or millimeter increment mandrels. Very few suppliers sell both millimeter and inch sizes. Some suppliers will convert their inch sizes to the closest millimeter equivalent, which is quite helpful. Always verify with your supplier what types of mandrels were used so that you know if you are getting inch sizes or millimeter sizes, as it may affect your projects.

Aspect ratio

Aspect ratio (AR) is the relationship between the wire gauge and the inner diameter (ID) of a ring. Here are some quick explanations of low versus high AR and how to use AR.
1. When a ring has a very low AR, it means the wire is quite thick and the ID is quite small, so there is limited amount room to weave more rings inside of a ring like this.
2. When a ring has a very high AR, the wire is thin and the ID is quite big, which means it may be unsuitable for many weaves because the rings are so thin and large that many weaves are floppy and cannot hold their shape.
3. If you love making a particular weave and you want to know how you can make a micro or mega version, you'll need to know the AR of the rings used and you can then find other rings with the same ARs, but in the mini or mega size that you want. The photo below shows rings that all have the same AR. This is what the weave called Jens Pind 3 looks like in three different ring sizes.

Most chain mail suppliers have already figured out the AR of each ring for you, so you just need to reference their various charts or AR listings to find the right size.

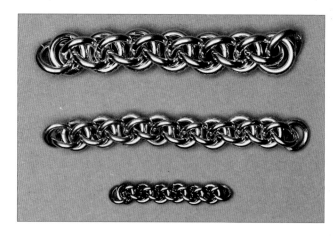

TOOLS

PLIERS

There are many available tools for chain mail. It is a myth to simply state that one plier brand/type is superior to another. I came to that conclusion after having used nearly every type of chain mail pliers available and realizing that pliers are made for particular "jobs" and each has benefits that serve the function of that job. Yes, I use Lindstrom and Tronex, which are some of the more expensive plier brands, but they are used for specific purposes, and definitely not the "best" pliers. There is no such thing as "the best." I use cheap pliers for specific purposes simply because I like the shape of thickness of the jaw or I like the way the spring tension feels in my hand.

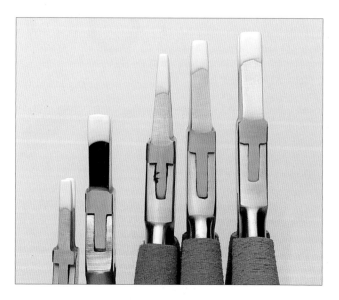

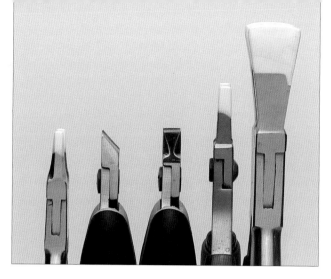

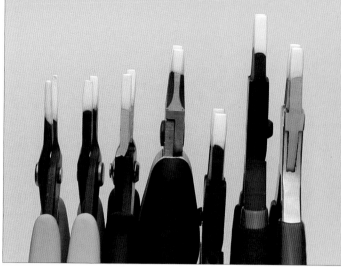

Ask yourself the following questions when you pick your first few sets of pliers. Check with your local bead store or chain mail supplier to see if you can try out the pliers before buying them.

- Do they fit in the palm of your hand comfortably?
- Are the handles a good length for your hand size?
- Is the spring tension good for your hand pressure?
- Is the jaw type appropriate for the jump rings you are typically using or using for a particular project?
- Are the pliers ideal to handle manipulating thick wire or very thin wire?

See the list of pliers on p. 12 for my recommendations. They all have smooth jaws (no teeth) and filed edges for jewelry-making purposes. I'm not recommending that you go out and buy all of these pliers right now. It's just a working list so you can see the benefits at a glance. For beginners working with average ring sizes, pick up either of the first two types of pliers (or both) to get you going.

Tool Magic is a temporary coating you can add to the tips of pliers to prevent marring and scratching the ring, especially the colored finishes. Tool Magic provides a great grip on the rings, too!

Dip the tips of the pliers in and slowly pull them out of the dip. Set them down flat over the edge of a table to dry at least 2 hours for the first coat. Repeat for the second coat, making sure to let them dry a few hours before using. When the dip starts to come off, peel to remove and re-dip!

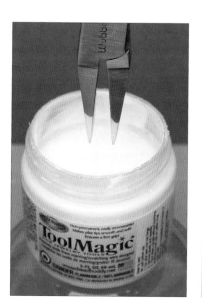

OTHER TOOLS

I use a **bead mat** or any soft surface where I can lay out my rings and beads without the fear of them rolling all over the place. You'll also want a **ruler** to measure your total desired length. I prefer a flexible measuring tape found in a fabric store. **A piece of wire** or even a thin twist tie can help hold the spot where your next ring goes and also help lead the path of the next ring.

You'll definitely need a pair of **cutters** to cut wire, and if by chance a particular weave doesn't go as planned, you can cut out the rings instead of un-weaving them.

If you have them, **fingernails** will come in handy! Fingernails are great for holding small beads in place, pushing rings into a specific position, and holding your weave steady.

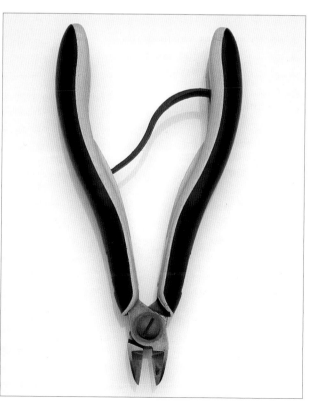

Pliers	Description
Ergo flatnose (any basic flatnose)	Small to medium size rings that are light to medium gauge in thickness. Thin jaws help you get into tight spaces, while allowing a good grip on the rings.
Ultra Ergo flatnose	Small to medium-large rings that are medium to heavy gauge in thickness. The wider handles allow for great stability and can be more comfortable in larger hands.
Xuron 485 FN flatnose	For light gauge rings that are small to medium in size. These are great for getting into a deeper section of weave to fix an error or to use on very small rings to get a good closure without the plier tips in the way and blocking your view.
Xuron KX48 flatnose	For light gauge rings that are small in size. Helpful for closing thin and tiny rings.
Hi-tech flatnose	Less expensive version of the Xuron brand. Comfortable grip.
Lindstrom RX7490 flatnose	Great for arthritic hands. Small to medium size rings that are light to medium gauge in thickness. Comfortable grip with adjustable spring tension. Very thin jaws are great for getting into tight areas. Also great for closing tiny rings.
Tronex 744 flatnose	Quite comfortable grip for medium to heavy gauge work. These are very strong pliers. The tension on these can be adjusted by the manufacturer. Thin and strong jaws for thicker rings in tight spaces.
Wubbers Classic Narrow flatnose	Cushion grip with slightly longer than average handles for medium to heavy gauge work. Narrow nose gives you strength on small to medium size rings.
Wubbers Classic Medium flatnose	Cushion grip with slightly longer than average handles for medium to heavy gauge work. Medium nose is helpful for almost all types of rings providing a steady grip.
Wubbers Classic Wide flatnose	Cushion grip with slightly longer than average handles for medium to heavy gauge work. Wide jaws are great for medium to large size rings while providing a firm grip.
Wubbers Apprentice flatnose	Molded grip that is very comfortable even without matching the grooves of your fingers. Same jaw as the Wubbers Wide nose, but handles are not as long.
Wubbers Baby Wubbers flatnose	Cushion grip with shorter than average handles for light to medium gauge work. Great for smaller hands and rings up through medium size.
Lindstrom squat flatnose	Durable plier for thicker medium size rings. Great for arthritic hands due to the comfortable grip and adjustable spring tension.
Lindstrom snub flatnose	Durable plier for thicker medium size rings. Great for arthritic hands due to the comfortable grip and adjustable spring tension.
Duckbill nose	Longer handles, like the Wubbers. These are specifically made for large to extra-large rings only.
Roundnose	Great for pulling rubber rings through other rubber rings.
Chainnose*	Great for pulling rubber rings through other rubber rings.
Bent chainnose*	Great for pulling rubber rings through other rubber rings.
Basic flatnose	Found via craft stores or online. Great for light to medium gauge rings.

*I do not use chainnose and bent chainnose pliers to weave chain mail. Why? I actually learned using these pliers and I never knew at that time why I found them to be so slippery and why it was hard to grasp the rings sometimes. When I tried flatnose pliers for the first time, I had a glorious epiphany: "Oh my goodness, I have the best grip EVER on these rings and they are hardly slippery at all!" The flatnose pliers provided a wider surface area grip on what I was weaving, and if I held them just right, the pliers were not in the way of my work. Please use whatever feels most comfortable for you.

TECHNIQUES

OPENING AND CLOSING JUMP RINGS

When you are opening and closing jump rings, you are engaging your shoulders, full arms, and hands. Think about your shoulders first. They do the work to push your arms where they need to move. Your arms then do work to twist your wrists and allow your fingers to grip firmly. If only your wrists and hands move, then you will feel some pain rather quickly. See "Relaxing your body while weaving," p. 15, for techniques to help calm your muscles.

Opening jump rings

Opening a jump ring properly is just as important as closing it well. It cannot be open too little (first ring) or too wide (third ring) **(a, b)**. The ideal opening takes practice and also depends on the weave. You want a decent "hook" to be able to scoop up a few rings and see where the hook is moving as you are weaving **(c)**.

1. To open a ring properly, first decide what pliers will fit on the ring, provide a good grip, and allow you to manipulate the wire with minimal strain. If you are right-handed, it is helpful to always pull the right-side of the ring in toward your body. If you are left-handed, pull the left-side of the ring in toward your body **(d)**. Doing this allows you to easily pick up the rings in your pliers with your dominant hand. It doesn't matter which side of the raw ring is already facing your body.
2. With a steady grip on both sides of the ring, slightly flick your dominant-hand's wrist back toward your body **(e, f)**. While you are opening the jump ring, you can also begin the closing process by very slightly pressing each side of the ring inward toward the center of the ring.

Closing jump rings

Perfecting closures showcases your finished pieces in a professional light. Closing rings takes much more practice then opening rings. 18-gauge base metal (try anodized aluminum, copper, or aluminum) rings in a medium size work well for practice. When working with very strong metals like steel, bronze, and brass, engage your whole upper body to minimize stress on your joints.
1. To close a ring properly, decide what pliers will do the job best.
2. Gain a steady grip on each side of the ring **(g)**. I like a slightly diagonal grip to get the most surface area of the pliers on each side of the ring as possible, without the pliers' jaws touching each other (See Troubleshooting, p. 14). Although the pliers grab the diagonal portions of the ring, your pliers should be in alignment with your ring, forming a straight line when viewing it from the top of the ring **(h)**.

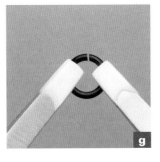

These alternate grips on the ring are also OK as long as you use even pressure with both hands to manipulate the rings. Make sure the tips of your pliers fit the ring well to avoid warping the ring **(i, j)**.

3. Slightly open the ring as normal (right or left-handed) and push the ends in very slightly toward each other. The ring has to be open to close it. It cannot be pushed to a quick close from the raw position **(k)**.

4. Push the dominant-hand side of the ring back down toward the other side of the ring. The two ends of the ring should now overlap each other slightly **(l)**.

5. Push the dominant-hand side of the ring past the other end, trying to scrape the ends past each other **(m)**. You may hear a slight scraping sound or a click, which is want you want.

6. Bring the non-dominant hand side of the ring in toward your body **(n, o)**. We have to overlap the non-dominant side over the original side that moved to ensure we achieve a flatter ring.

7. Again, bring the two ends together, pushing them slightly inward to scrape the ends and achieve a tight closure. Check to see how well the ring is closed with your finger, and look at it from the top to ensure it is not offset. Check it from the side to make sure there is no hairline opening **(p)**.

TIP:

Try NOT to move each side of the ring back and forth a bunch of times. If you manipulate the ring too much, you may twist it out of shape and possibly break it. Work-hardening is not necessary for chain mail because the rings are already made quite strong. Aim to achieve a good closure with minimal movements; it'll save time and reduce hand and wrist strain in the long run!

  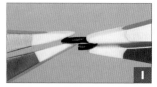 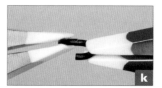

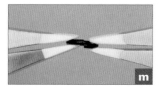   

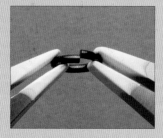   

Troubleshooting

Watch how the pliers are gripping the ring from the opening through the closing steps. Sometimes the pliers may move, tilt, slant away from or toward you, touch each other and more. The following are things to watch out for and how to trouble-shoot fixing rings that aren't closed properly.

Pliers grip the ring perpendicularly: Even though this grip is OK, when the pliers are too small for the ring, the ring can easily be warped because the surface area covering the ring on each side is uneven and you have less control over each side.

Pliers grabbing/ touching each other too low on the ring: There is almost no leverage to close the ring properly and if your pliers touch, the ring may not move at all.

A hairline opening occurs when there is not enough overlap on each side of the ring during the closing process. Remember that each side of the ring should slightly overlap each other to eliminate the gap.

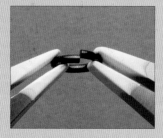

Pliers pushing out away from or pushing in toward your body: This grip results in a pringle or saddle-shaped ring.

One pair of pliers is angled perpendicularly in toward or out away from your body: This grip may result in the pliers slipping off of the ring and also warping the ring out of its circle shape.

Pliers touching in the middle: Ring will likely become warped or will not be able to move. An **overbite** is when one side of the ring is higher than the other. This can occur because of a number of grip issues or maybe one hand is just much stronger than the other. You can fix an overbite by slightly re-opening the ring, holding the side of the ring that is higher steady and then re-closing the ring, while pulling the lower side up just slightly to meet the higher side. Fixing these rings takes lots of practice and not all rings with an overbite can be fixed, as they may have been pulled too far out of the circle shape.

Pringled or saddle-shaped rings are usually the result of both pliers angling out away from or in toward your body while closing. Make sure your grip is straight in alignment with the ring.

When the ends of each side of the ring don't match up flush, it is called an off-set ring. Hold one side steady and slightly push or pull the other side of the ring until it lines up. Metals such as aluminum and steel have lots of spring back, so you have to push or pull against the spring back, more than you might think, in order for the ring to spring back to the proper alignment with the other side for a seamless closure.

OTHER TECHNIQUES

These time-saving tips help you weave like a pro—and also help with dexterity and maybe even minimize accidentally dropping your work while weaving.

Your hand pressure while gripping the pliers has to be firm, but gentle. It takes practice to feel what works best so that your hands, wrists and arms do not tire so quickly. Try not to grip the pliers so hard that your knuckles are stretched and pale. When you grip this hard, you may slip on the rings while trying to close them and possibly drop your piece. You need to grip firmly when closing the ring; just be careful that it is not too firm. Essentially, your hands should not hurt and your fingernails should not be digging into and scratching your palms. The photos show a firm, but gentle way of gripping the pliers to minimize strain **(a, b)**.

Keep your pliers in your hands at all times while weaving. When you keep your pliers in your hands and tuck them into the crook of your thumb and forefinger, you save a whole lot of time because you are not putting them down and picking them up again after every action. Your pinchers (the forefinger

and thumb of your non-dominant hand) can help you hold the weave steady and adjust rings picked up by the pliers so you can weave them more easily **(c)**.

Insert the rings as if you were throwing a frisbee. Imagine how you hold a frisbee and flick it across away from your body. Try holding the pliers with your open ring that way and weaving it in your piece from this slightly horizontal hand position. With the hook pointing away and slightly down, you can easily weave the ring into the proper position. There are instances where this hand position cannot be used, but when you can, do it! It'll help reduce strain on your wrist.

Finishing a pre-made chain

Each end of the chain has a tiny ⅛" 18-gauge ring. On one end of this tiny ring, I add the lobster claw. On the opposite end, I add a ³⁄₁₆" 18-gauge ring for the lobster claw to hook onto. Feel free to add a larger ring here if desired.

Relaxing your body while weaving

When you are weaving, consider how your posture and movements are affecting your body. Sit up in a semi-firm chair with back support, lumbar support, and a decent cushion. Your work surface should not be too high where you are creating stress on your shoulders or too low, causing you to bend over frequently. Your elbows should remain in a relaxed, slightly bent position. The way you sit and how your body is positioned will make a huge difference. When possible, try to keep your head from looking downward and keep it level with the horizon, remembering to look forward and not down when closing your jump rings. Your wrists and forearms should be doing most of the work once you master the proper grip on the pliers. Your grip should be firm, but not too firm so as to cause shaking or stress on the rings.

Cleaning and care

Take care of your beautiful jewelry and you can wear it for many years. Try to avoid wearing your jewelry excessively in water, especially salt water, which will deteriorate most metals. Also keep jewelry away from household chemicals. When you are not wearing your jewelry, store it in plastic ziplock baggies or other air-tight containers. Even aluminum and steel can become dull due to oxidation. For tarnishable metals, insert an anti-tarnish tab or strip in a small sealed plastic bag or container, which helps to reduce tarnish.

Storage caddies are a great idea for organizing your rings, and they can also be used to store your finished jewelry. I have a large, velvet-lined train case with many shelves that fold out. It closes up nearly air tight.

Tumbling

There are many methods for cleaning rings and also for cleaning your finished jewelry pieces. My favorite method for most of my jewelry is using a rotary tumbler. The tumbling method works for nearly all jewelry in this book (except anodized aluminum). For alternative cleaning methods, please see the final column of suggestions.

Materials

- Rotary tumbler **(a)**
- Single or double rubber barrels with watertight lids
- Liquid burnishing compound
- ¾ capful for each barrel
- Stainless steel shot **(b)** (add half a handful or slightly more—barrel should feel heavy with shot in it)
- Blow dryer or fan
- Kitchen towels
- Fine mesh strainer
- Hot water (For aluminum and steel)
- Cold water (For copper, brass, bronze, and sterling)

1. Place a few pieces of jewelry in the tumbler. Be careful about adding multiple items that may tangle **(c)**.
2. Add the steel shot. This is called "jewelry mix" because it has three different sizes of shot that get in between all the small areas.

3. Add the liquid burnishing compound. You can also use unscented mild dish soap like Dawn, but it may corrode your shot over time.
4. Add water to fill the remaining ½ to ¾ of the barrel **(d)**.
5. Add your lids and set the barrels on the tumbler. Even if you fill only one barrel, it is a good idea to add the empty barrel on the tumbler to even out the weight a bit.
6. Tumble for 15 to 30 minutes.
7. Remove from the tumbler and rinse the items in a strainer **(e)**.
8. Put on a towel and blow dry them right away. Metals containing copper must be dried quickly on a cool setting to prevent permanent tarnish. (I rub them with my hand and move them around under the hair dryer until they are completely dry.)

For aluminum and stainless steel, put hot water and dish soap in a very strong, watertight plastic sealed container. Shake it or rotate it gently for a few minutes. Rinse and dry thoroughly.

Dip **metals that contains copper** in distilled vinegar. Don't let them sit in vinegar, as the acids will eat away at the metal. Wash off the vinegar with cool water and dish soap. Dry immediately with a blow dryer on the cool setting.

Rinse **silicone rubber jewelry** in water and use Armor All to condition it. Rubber can dry and even crack over time, so conditioning it keeps it moisturized and shiny. Simply spray just a tiny bit on a white towel or directly on the jewelry. Pat dry. Do not rinse the Armor All off.

Enameled copper can be tumbled and dipped in vinegar without affecting the finish. **Anodized aluminum cannot be tumbled!** You can only clean it very gently with water and dish soap.

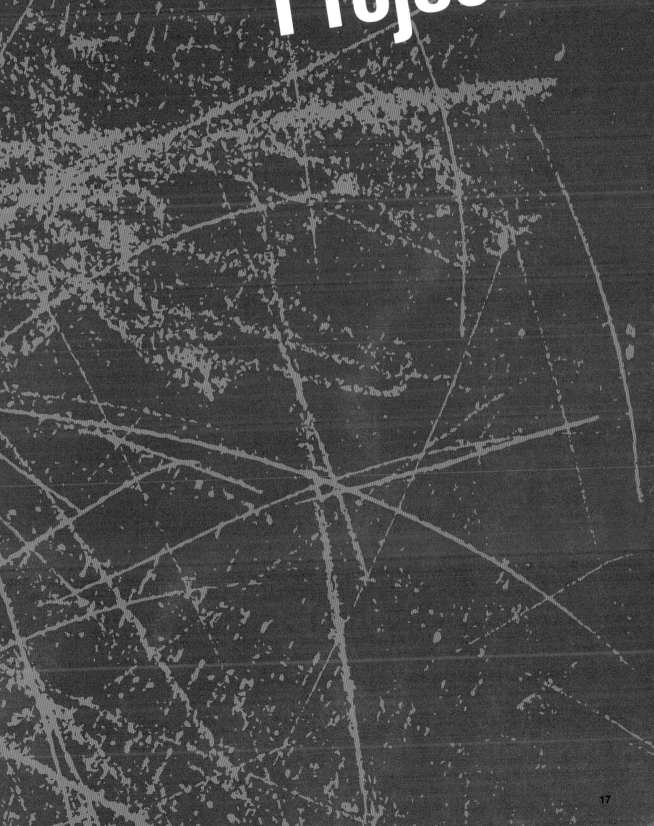

Projects

looped earrings

This quick and simple earring is made with two sizes of glass rings. Imagine the color possibilities!

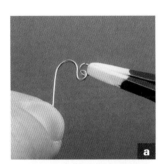

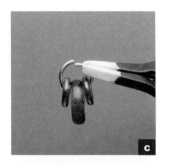

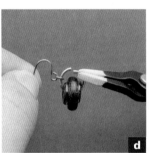

color option

Prep: Open all of the rings.

1. Add a tiny ring to the earring wire and close it **(a)**.

2. Weave a large ring through a large glass ring. Don't close the ring yet **(b)**.

3. Add a small glass ring on each side. Keep the ring open **(c)**.

4. Weave the large ring through the tiny ring attached to your earring wire. Close the large ring. In order to close these high AR rings seamlessly, extra overlap is needed on each side of the ring **(d–g)**.

5. Repeat to make another earring **(h)**.

looped drop earrings

A little-bit-longer variation of the "Looped Earring," p. 18, this project is still very easy— and quite beautiful.

Prep: Open all of the rings.

1. Add a tiny ring to the earring wire and close it. Repeat for the second earring wire **(a)**.

2. Weave a large ring through a large glass ring and one small glass ring. Don't close the ring yet **(b)**.

3. Before closing, weave the large ring through the tiny ring hanging from the earring wire. Now close the ring. Make sure the small glass ring is in the front of the earring **(c)**. Close the ring.

4. Add a small glass ring to a large ring and weave it through only the large glass ring. Close the ring **(d, e)**.

5. Repeat steps 2–4 for the second earring.

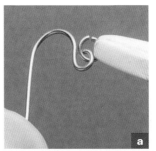

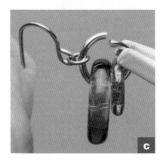

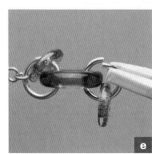

color
option

decadent confection bracelet

A well-known and popular weave originally known as Shaggy Loops, this bracelet feels and looks like glistening candy when using glass and beads. Hear the light rattle from the fringe as you wear it.

| REFERENCE | METAL/TYPE | QTY | RING SIZE | RING GAUGE | | AR |
				SWG	MM	
large ring	aluminum	19	5/16 in. (7.9mm)	18	1.2	7.1
glass ring	Czech glass, bronze iris	40	9–9.5mm OD	—	—	1.5–1.8
bead	6º seed beads, Miyuki, metallic brown iris	40	—	—	—	—
medium clasp ring	aluminum	3	3/16 in. (4.8mm)	18	1.2	4.1

rhodium-plated craftsman toggle clasp

Tools: 2 pairs of flatnose pliers
Length of Time: 2 hours or less

Prep: Open all of the rings.

1. Add two glass rings on to a large ring. Also add a glass bead to each side of the ring so they rest on top of the glass ring. Add one more glass ring, and close the ring **(a–d)**.
2. Add the toggle loop portion of the clasp to the single glass ring added last in the previous step by weaving a medium clasp ring to connect them **(e)**.
3. Separate the two hanging glass rings and weave a large ring through the previous large ring. Before closing, add a bead to each side of the ring and then add a glass ring to each side. Close the ring **(f–j)**.

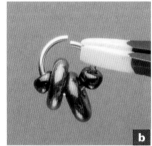

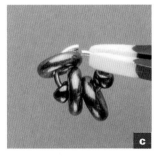

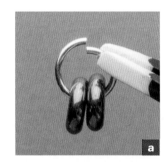

4. Repeat step 3 to complete the desired length. Finish the opposite end by adding an extra glass ring as in step 1 **(k)**.
5. Attach the bar half of the toggle clasp by repeating step 2 **(l)**, weaving a medium ring. If using the suggested toggle, no additional clasp rings are needed.

design option

Create matching earrings or a pendant by creating mini sections of the bracelet.

synthesis necklace

These spiraling flowers with glass accents blend together harmoniously to create a vintage-style necklace. This basic weave is known as *flowers* and comes from the spiral family of weaves. The technique shown is called Mobiusing. Most spiral weaves tend to make the entire piece spiral on its own due to the way the rings are woven. For this piece, each flower unit spirals in opposite directions to provide a necklace that resists twisting on its own.

You will need...

REFERENCE	METAL/TYPE	QTY	RING SIZE	RING GAUGE SWG	RING GAUGE MM	AR
large ring	anodized aluminum	80	5/16 in. (7.9mm)	18	1.2	7.1
medium ring	anodized aluminum	42	7/32 in. (5.6mm)	18	1.2	7.4
glass ring	Czech glass, white opal	21	9–9.5mm OD	—	—	1.5– 1.8
small clasp ring	anodized aluminum	3	3/16 in. (4.8mm)	18	1.2	4.1

matte black swivel lobster clasp

Tools: 2 pairs of flatnose pliers
Length of Time: 3–5 hours

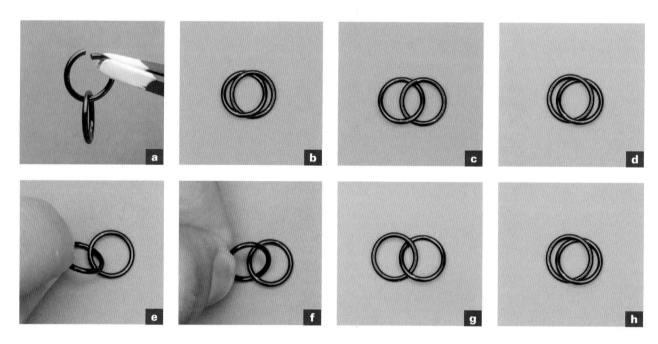

Prep: Close 20 of the large rings, and open the rest of the rings.

1. Add a large closed ring onto an open large ring. Close the ring **(a, b)**.

2. Repeat step 1, creating multiple units to complete your desired length. You will need approximately 20 units for an 18" necklace.

3. Take any single two-ring unit, lay the rings flat, and slightly separate them. Depending on which way they lie, you may notice that either the first ring (left-most) or the second ring (right-most) will be on a slight decline. **Photo c** shows the first ring pointing down on a decline away from your body. **Photo d** shows the second ring on a decline. The way that the first ring sits in relation to the second ring will indicate the direction of the spiral of the unit. These two-ring units are considered to be mobiused now—essentially spiraling through each other. **Photos b** and **d** show the start of two opposite spiraling units.

4. Slightly picking up the first ring and flipping it will change the direction of the swirl **(e–h)**. You will need to ensure that half of your two-ring flower units lie with the first ring matching **photo h** and the second half of your two-ring units match **photo b**.

5. Weave a new large ring in through the center of both of the rings in a unit that matches **photo h**. Weaving down through the unit helps to keep the direction of the spiral from changing position **(i–k)**.

6. This new ring should fit snugly in with the previous two rings and all rings should spiral in the same direction. If it is slightly jutting out from the unit, flip that ring over so they all form a blended spiral **(l–p)**.

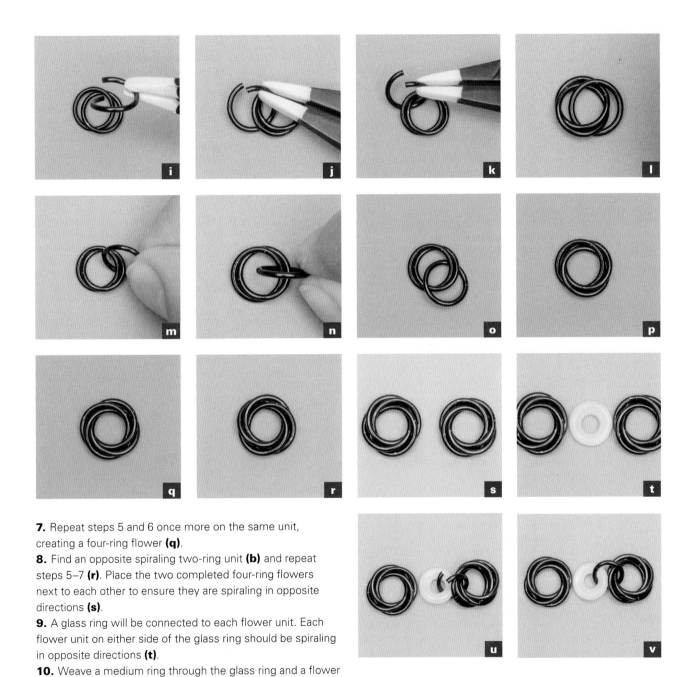

7. Repeat steps 5 and 6 once more on the same unit, creating a four-ring flower **(q)**.

8. Find an opposite spiraling two-ring unit **(b)** and repeat steps 5–7 **(r)**. Place the two completed four-ring flowers next to each other to ensure they are spiraling in opposite directions **(s)**.

9. A glass ring will be connected to each flower unit. Each flower unit on either side of the glass ring should be spiraling in opposite directions **(t)**.

10. Weave a medium ring through the glass ring and a flower unit. Close the ring **(u, v)**.

11. Weave a medium ring through the same glass ring and the other flower unit. Close the ring **(w)**.

12. Continue the pattern by adding a glass ring, an opposite spiraling unit, and then a glass ring again and so on until you reach the desired length **(x–z)**.

13. End your pattern with a glass ring at each end. Attach a lobster claw clasp with a small clasp ring to one end. At the opposite end, weave a single small clasp ring to the glass and then a final small clasp ring **(aa)**.

design option

oracle pendant

Listen to the oracle; she will provide great wisdom and guidance! This 1¼"-wide open and floral pattern showcases rubber and glass rings. You can also create lightweight statement earrings in a bunch of color variations! This pattern uses techniques from the Japanese style of weaving.

REFERENCE	METAL/TYPE	QTY	RING SIZE	RING GAUGE		AR
				SWG	MM	
extra-large ring	silicon rubber, black	1	25/64 in. (9.9mm)	14	2	5.4
large ring	aluminum	8	1/4 in. (6.4mm)	18	1.2	5.7
medium ring	anodized aluminum	8	3/16 in. (4.8mm)	18	1.2	4.1
glass ring	Czech glass ring, green iris	8	9.5mm OD	—	—	1.5
bead	6º seed beads, Miyuki, green iris	8	—	—	—	—
small clasp ring	aluminum	3	3/16 in. (4.8mm)	18	1.2	4.1
tiny clasp ring	aluminum	2	1/8 in. (3.2mm)	18	1.2	2.8
rhodium-plated swivel lobster claw clasp						
pre-made aluminum chain (desired length)						

Tools: 2 pairs of flatnose pliers
Length of Time: 1 hour or less

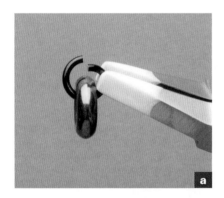

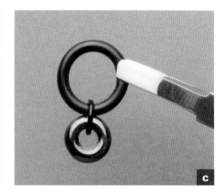

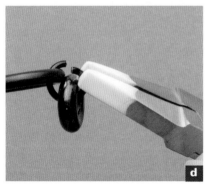

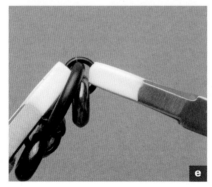

Prep: Open all of the rings.

1. Add a glass ring on to a medium jump ring ring and weave it around the rubber ring. Close the ring **(a–c)**.

2. Repeat step 1, weaving around the same rubber ring. You will need to firmly pull the rubber ring onto the open medium ring to find room to close it. The medium ring with the glass ring on it should fit very snug around the rubber ring **(d, e)**.

3. Repeat step 2 six times for a total of eight glass rings snugly attached to the rubber ring **(f)**.

4. Weave a large ring through any glass ring. Add a bead to the large ring and weave it down through the adjacent glass ring. Close the ring **(g–k)**.

5. Repeat step 4 seven times, each time starting your new large ring by going through one glass ring already connected

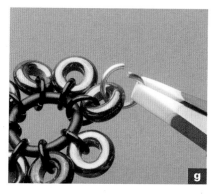

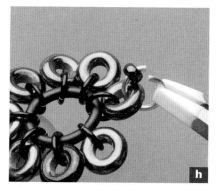

tip Thicker glass rings work well for this project because a very snug fit is required. If you want to use thinner glass rings, you may need to substitute the medium rings for a slightly smaller size jump ring.

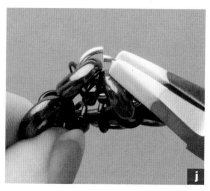

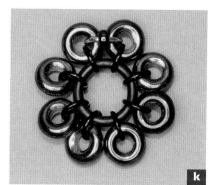

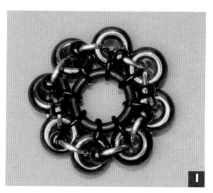

by a large ring and also a new glass ring. You will make a complete circle of connected glass rings **(l)**.

6. Attached a pre-made chain with two small clasp rings (same size as the medium rings from the project) **(m)**.

7. Finish by adding a lobster claw clasp to the chain by adding a tiny clasp ring on one side of the clasp. On the opposite end of the pre-made chain, add a tiny ring and then end on a small clasp ring. Refer to the "Finishing a pre-made chain" section on p. 15.

color option

ninja star earrings

Watch out! These little star cuties are coming right at you! They remind me of the ninja stars thrown in martial arts, except actual ninja stars have either four or six points, not five.

| REFERENCE | METAL/TYPE | QTY | RING SIZE | RING GAUGE | | AR |
				SWG	MM	
large ring	anodized aluminum	2	5/16 in. (7.9mm)	16	1.6	5.4
large rubber ring	silicone rubber, red	10	5/16 in. (7.9mm)	14	2	3.9
small rubber ring	silicone rubber, orange	10	1/8 in. (3.2mm)	14	2	1.7
tiny clasp ring	anodized aluminum	2	5/32 in. (4mm)	18	1.2	3.6

pair of black niobium earring wires

Tools: Pair of bentnose, chainnose, or roundnose pliers, and 2 pairs of flatnose pliers made for handling 16-gauge wire
Length of Time: 1 hour or less

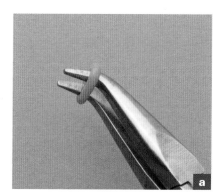

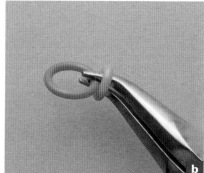

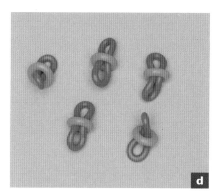

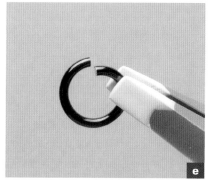

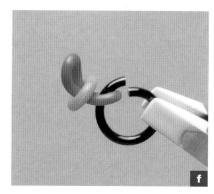

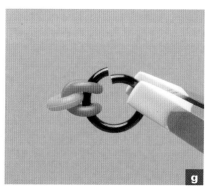

Prep: Open the large rings.

1. Using the chainnose, roundnose, or bentnose pliers, roll a small rubber ring over the tip of the jaws **(a)**.
2. Insert a large rubber ring into the plier tips and then roll the small rubber ring across the large rubber ring so that it sits evenly in the middle **(b, c)**.
3. Repeat steps 1 and 2 four times to create mini rubber units **(d)**.
4. Fold and slide both loops of a rubber unit onto the large jump ring **(e–g)**. Do not close the ring yet.

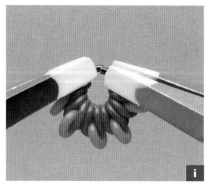
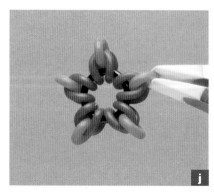

5. Repeat step 4 with the remaining rubber units. Smoosh the rubber rings down under the pliers to find room to close the ring **(h, i)**.

6. Tug gently on the "arms" of the star shape to straighten them and make them pointed **(j)**.

7. Attach a tiny ring to any point on the star and add your earring wire. Close the ring.

8. Repeat to make another earring. To make the "arms" resist moving along the large ring, you can weave a second large jump ring parallel to the first one.

color option

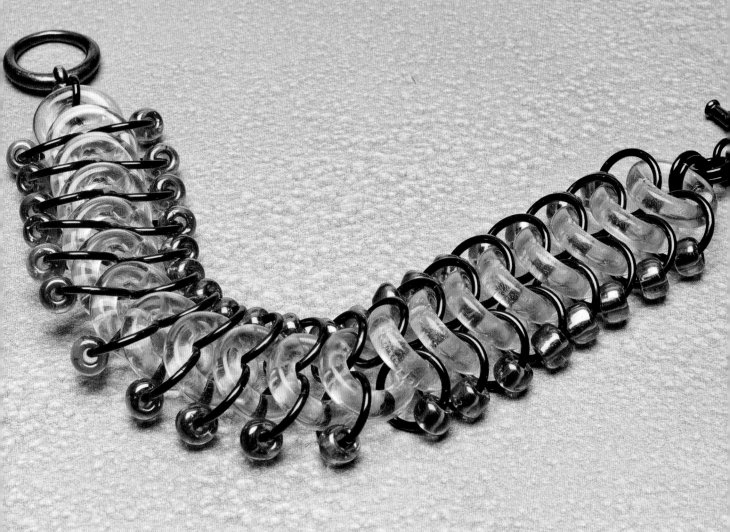

arched ascent bracelet

This is a variation of one of the oldest and most popular chain mail weaves known as European 4-in-1. This pattern showcases a modernized version with large, gorgeous glass rings and large seed beads. This bracelet measures about 1" wide.

| REFERENCE | METAL/TYPE | QTY | RING SIZE | RING GAUGE | | AR |
				SWG	MM	
large ring	anodized aluminum	58	5/16 in. (7.9mm)	18*	1.2	5.4
glass ring	Czech glass, light rose	25	14mm OD	—	—	2.2
bead	3⁰ seed beads, Toho, transparent rainbow gray	58	—	—	—	—
medium clasp ring	anodized aluminum	3	7/32 in. (5.6mm)	18	1.2	7.4
tiny clasp ring	anodized aluminum	3	5/32 in. (4mm)	18	1.2	3.6
gunmetal-plated toggle clasp						

Tools: 2 pairs of flatnose pliers
Length of Time: 2 hours or less

* You can also use 5/16" 16-gauge (1.6mm) large rings.

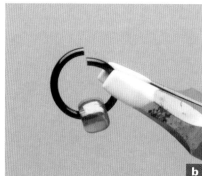

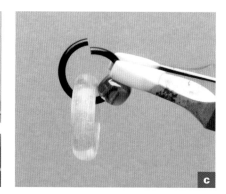

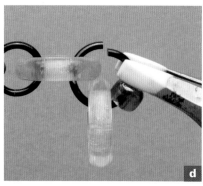

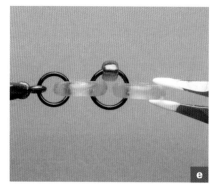

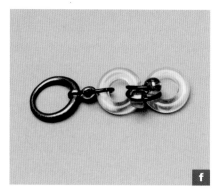

Prep: Open all of the rings.

1. Connect the loop part of the toggle to a glass ring with a medium clasp ring **(a)**.

2. Add a bead and a glass ring to a large ring. Ensure they are added in this order **(b–e)**. Before closing, weave through the first glass ring connected to your clasp.

3. Weave a second large ring with a bead through both of the same glass rings. Ensure that both beads are sitting on the same side of the glass rings **(f)**.

4. Flip the last glass ring behind the first glass ring, allowing it to sit behind the rings with beads. Move the rings with beads to each side of the glass rings **(g–j)**.

5. Add a glass ring and then a bead to a large ring (the opposite order of step 2). Weave it through the front side of the previous glass ring and then close the ring. The photos show a front view and also a side view of the path of this ring **(k–m)**.

6. Weave a large ring through the final two glass rings, parallel to the previous large ring with a bead. Before closing, add a bead, ensuring that it sits on the same side of the glass rings as the previous beaded ring. Close the ring **(n–p)**.

7. Flip the hanging glass ring behind the previous glass ring as in step 4. Move the rings with beads to each side of the glass rings **(q, r)**.

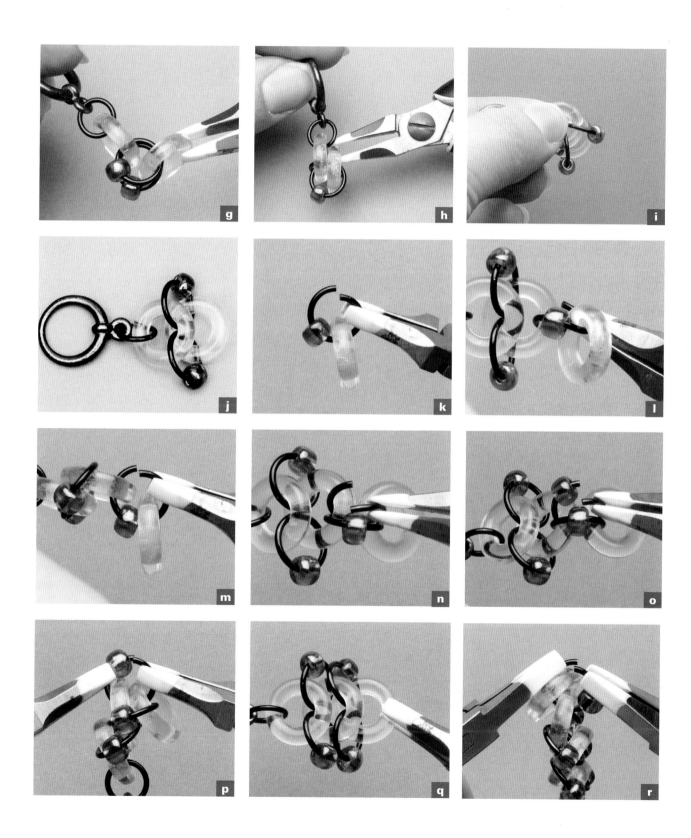

8. Repeat steps 5–7 to complete the desired length. Always ensure you are weaving the rings from the same direction of the bracelet and that the beads stay on the same side of the glass rings.

9. Add two medium clasp rings to the final glass ring. Add two tiny clasp rings to the medium rings. Add a final tiny ring to the previous pair of tiny rings and also connect it to the bar half of the toggle clasp **(u, v)**.

tip You will know if you have woven any large rings incorrectly when the bead is locked inside of the center of the glass ring, instead of falling loosely to the outer edge of the large jump rings **(s, t)**.

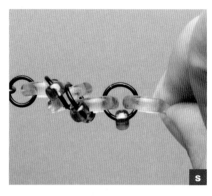

s

t

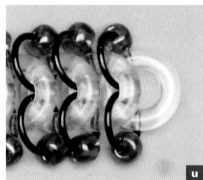

u

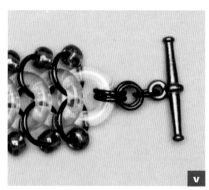

v

color **option**

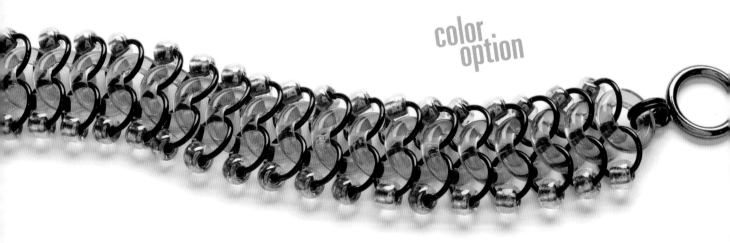

parallel bars bracelet

Create this glass variation of the popular European 4-in-1 weave with just a few rings. This project can be done quite quickly once you get the hang of repeatedly reversing the direction of the weave.

REFERENCE	METAL/TYPE	QTY	RING SIZE	RING GAUGE		AR
				SWG	MM	
large ring	anodized aluminum	18	3/8 in. (9.5mm)	16	1.6	6.5
glass ring	Czech glass, Capri blue	12	9–9.5mm OD	—	—	1.5–1.8
bead	6º seed beads, Miyuki, gunmetal	31	—	—	—	—
small clasp ring	anodized aluminum	4	3/16 in. (4.8mm)	18	1.2	4.1
tiny clasp ring	anodized aluminum	2–4	5/32 in. (4mm)	18	1.2	3.6
gunmetal-plated toggle clasp						

Tools: 2 pairs of flatnose pliers made for handling 16-gauge wire
Length of Time: 2 hours or less

tip You may substitute 18-gauge rings (which are not as durable, due to high AR) if the beads are not fitting on the 16-gauge rings. Beads on 16-gauge rings make for a very snug fit. Not all bead holes are identical, as they vary from batch to batch, so you may have to go through a few to find ones that fit correctly.

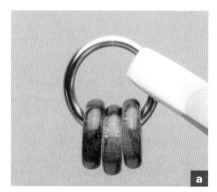

a

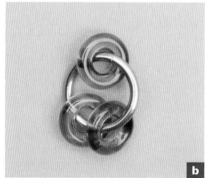

b

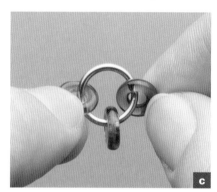

c

d

e

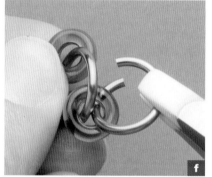

f

g

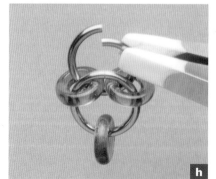

h

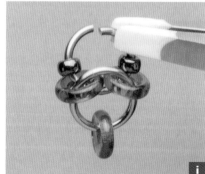

i

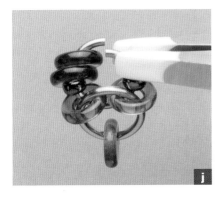

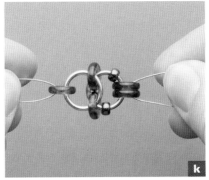

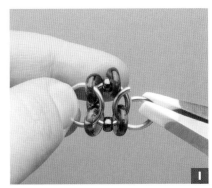

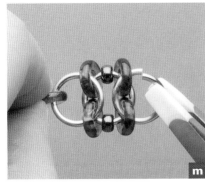

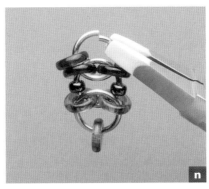

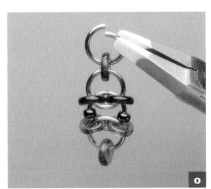

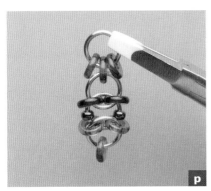

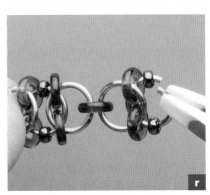

Prep: Open all of the rings.

1. Add three glass rings to a large ring and close the ring **(a)**.

2. Separate the glass rings so one ring is at the top of the large ring **(b)**.

3. Separate the two hanging glass rings to each side of the large ring as if you were opening the pages of a book. Pinch them with your thumb in your non-dominant hand to hold them in place **(c–e)**.

4. Weave a large ring down through the glass ring closest to your body and then up through the one further away. Do not close the ring yet **(f–h)**.

5. Add a glass bead to each side of the open ring and re-grip the ring with your pliers above the beads. Also add two glass rings and close the large ring **(i–k)**.

6. Separate the hanging glass rings as in step 3 to each side of the large ring. This time, weave a large ring up through the glass ring closest to your body (this is opposite of how you started weaving in step 4) and continue weaving down through the glass ring further away from you. Don't close the ring yet **(l, m)**.

7. Before closing, add a single glass ring. Close the ring **(n)**.

8. Weave a large ring through the single glass ring and add two glass rings. Close the ring **(o, p)**.

9. Repeat steps 3–8 to continue creating the desired length **(q–w)**.

tip Each time you add two glass rings, you will need to open them up like the pages of a book, and add two glass beads and two glass rings before you can close the large ring. There is a single separator ring in between each section of four glass rings with beads.

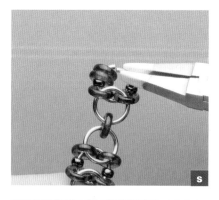 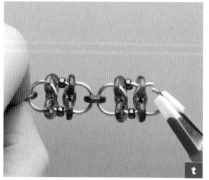 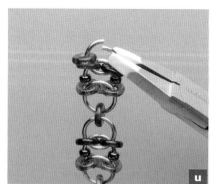

 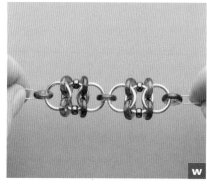 

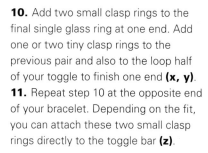  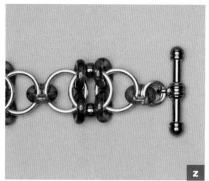

10. Add two small clasp rings to the final single glass ring at one end. Add one or two tiny clasp rings to the previous pair and also to the loop half of your toggle to finish one end **(x, y)**.

11. Repeat step 10 at the opposite end of your bracelet. Depending on the fit, you can attach these two small clasp rings directly to the toggle bar **(z)**.

color
option

to the point earrings

The small glass looks like it is floating inside the center of these earrings that form a defined point at the bottom. It can be a bit tricky to get the beads into the right spot due to the proper form needed in the center section of the earrings.

REFERENCE	METAL/TYPE	QTY	RING SIZE	RING GAUGE		AR
				SWG	MM	
large **thick** ring	aluminum	4	3/8 in. (9.5mm)	16	1.6	6.5
large **thin** ring	aluminum	2	3/8 in. (9.5mm)	18	1.2	8.6
medium ring	aluminum	4	21/64 in. (8.3mm)	18	1.2	9.1
large glass ring	Czech glass rings, amethyst	2	14mm OD	—	—	1.5–1.8
small glass ring	Czech glass rings, lilac	2	9–9.5mm OD	—	—	2.5
bead	6⁰ seed beads, Miyuki, violet gold luster	4	—	—	—	—
tiny clasp ring	aluminum	2	1/8 in. (3.2mm)	18	1.2	2.8

pair of surgical steel earring wires

Tools: 2 pairs of flatnose pliers that can handle 16- and 18-gauge wire
Length of Time: 1 hour or less

color option

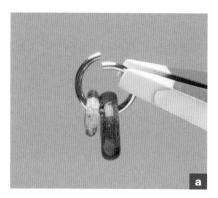

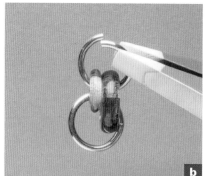

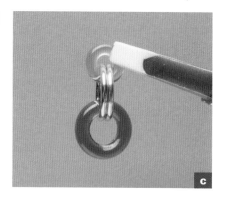

Prep: Open all of the rings.

1. Add a large and a small glass ring to a large **thick** ring. Close the ring **(a)**.

2. Weave a large **thick** ring through the two glass rings. Close the ring **(b)**.

3. Separate the glass rings so that the two large **thick** rings are parallel **(c)**.

4. Holding the piece by the large glass ring, begin to insert a large **thin** ring in between the two large **thick** rings, but do not go all the way through to the other side of these large **thick** rings. Only weave the large **thin** ring in so far as to just pick up or scoop the top large **thick** ring **(d)**.

5. Add two beads to the large **thin** ring **(e)**.

6. Push the hook of your large **thin** ring slightly down to continue weaving through the other side of the large **thick** rings. It will feel a bit tight and tricky to get through here. You will need to make sure that as you are pushing the **thin** ring through, that one bead sits on each side of the large glass ring. The large **thin** ring also slides underneath the small glass ring. Close the ring **(f–i)**.

tip
At this stage, the bead may travel outside of where it should be. In order to get the bead back inside the center of the large **thick** rings, bend the large glass ring back to loosen up the tension in the center of the earring. Gently slide the bead back into the center and then bend the large glass ring down to its original position **(j–l)**.

7. Weave a medium ring directly above a bead on one side of the small glass ring. This medium ring should go through both large **thick** rings and the large **thin** ring and continue around to encircle the top portion of the large **thin** ring. Close the ring **(m–o)**.

8. Repeat step 7 with a medium ring, starting the path directly above the second bead and continuing all the way through **(p)**.

9. Add a tiny clasp ring joining the two medium rings and also add the earring wire.

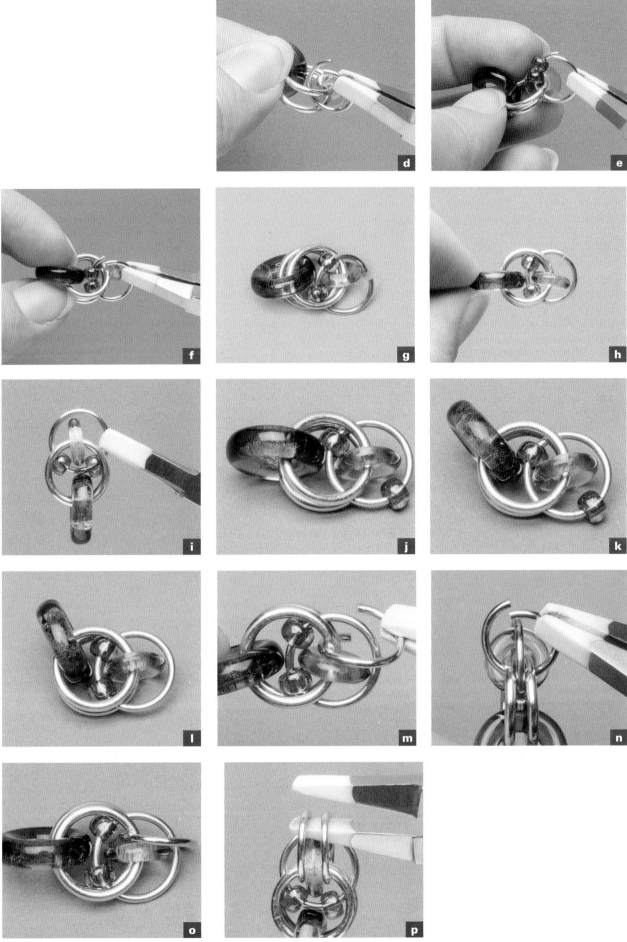

celtic crossroads bracelet

The Celtic Visions weave makes a rejuvenated appearance in this pattern with both large and small glass rings. The units are flipped 90 degrees and connected horizontally, which reminds me of a cross walk. This statement bracelet measures about 1" wide and features a large artisan-style toggle clasp. The large glass rings resist overlapping onto each other.

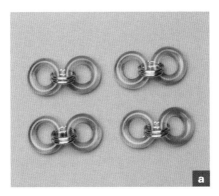

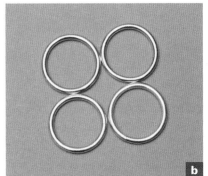

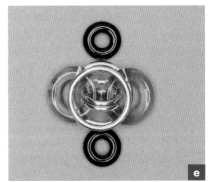

Prep: Close the extra-large rings. Open all of the other rings.

1. Create 6–10 units (depending on your total desired length) that contain two large glass rings connected together by two large jump rings. You will need seven of these units for a finished length of 7" **(a)**.

2. Make sure you have your closed extra-large rings ready. You'll need two for every glass ring unit you create in step 1 **(b)**.

3. Lay an extra-large closed ring on top of the glass ring unit encircling the connector rings **(c)**.

4. Place another extra-large closed ring underneath the glass ring unit, encircling the same connector rings **(d)**.

5. In the following steps you will be attaching a small glass ring each to the top and bottom of the unit. This is a preview of where the small glass rings will be joined **(e)**.

6. On one side of the glass ring unit, weave a large ring through the two extra-large rings and large glass ring that is sitting in between them. Before closing, also add a small glass ring. Close the ring. Adjust your piece on a flat surface so that the extra-large rings rest on each side of the glass rings. Also push the small glass ring to rest above the center

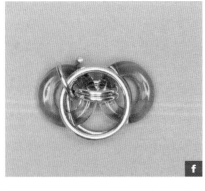

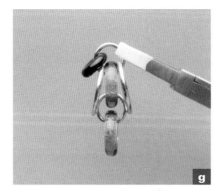

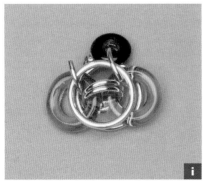

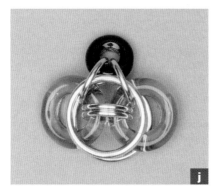

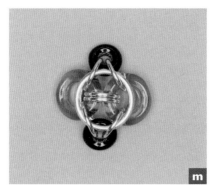

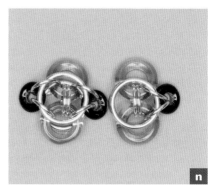

of the glass ring unit. It doesn't matter if the orientation of the ring you just closed is on the other side of the unit because you will fill in the other side in the next step **(f–h)**.

7. Repeat step 6, except do not add a small glass ring. Weave it through the path directly adjacent to the previous ring you just closed. Depending on which way your piece is facing after you adjusted it on the flat surface, it may look like this ring is woven in the exact same place as previous step. Before closing, weave through the small glass ring. Close the ring **(i, j)**.

![tip] There is a very limited amount of space to close this second ring when weaving through the small glass ring. Start closing your ring by putting one pair of pliers just inside the small glass ring to grip it. Once you get it closed a bit, move that same pair of pliers higher up above the glass and almost at a 45-degree angle to find enough room on the ring to grab it and close it **(k, l)**.

8. Repeat steps 6 and 7 at the bottom of the same glass ring unit. This is the start of your bracelet and the only unit that has glass rings attached at both ends prior to joining the units in the final steps **(m)**.

9. Repeat steps 3–7 to create additional units that have only one small glass ring attached at the top of the large glass rings (see **photo j**).

10. With large jump rings, connect the completed units from step 9 to each other following the paths from step 8 **(n–p)**.

11. In the following steps you will be attaching additional small glass rings in between each large glass ring unit.

Photo q shows where the small glass rings will be placed.

12. Weave two medium rings connecting a large glass ring and a newly added small glass ring **(r)**.

13. Weave two medium rings connecting the newly added small glass ring to the adjacent large glass ring. There is barely any extra room for this small glass ring to move around once it is connected to the second large glass ring. It is a snug fit **(s)**.

o

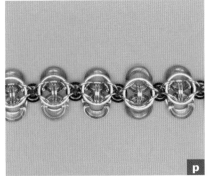

p

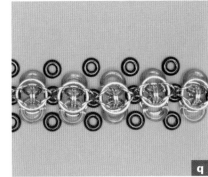

q

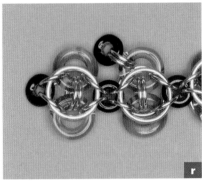

r

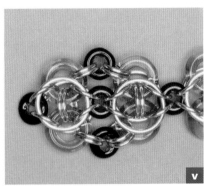

s

t

u

v

w

x

tip Closing the rings in step 13 is difficult because you are pulling them across to the adjacent large glass ring and it is a tight squeeze. To get these medium rings closed properly, you will need to slightly overlap the large glass ring on to the small to find more room to grasp the ring. You can also turn the weave over and overlap the small glass ring on to the large glass ring to gain room **(t, u)**.

14. Repeat steps 12 and 13 on the lower portion of the same large glass ring units **(v)**.

15. Repeat steps 12–14 down the length of your bracelet. Leave about 2" of length for your large toggle clasp.

16. Add the loop part of your toggle to one end by attaching it with two small clasp rings **(w)**.

17. At the opposite end of your bracelet, attach a small glass ring to the last one with two medium rings. Add the bar half of the toggle clasp by attaching it to the final glass ring with two small clasp rings **(x)**.

caterpillar earrings

Why are these called Caterpillar Earrings? Because they are a variation from my bracelet design, the Glass Caterpillar shown in the introduction section. These dainty and fun earrings dangle just a bit below the ear.

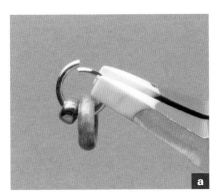

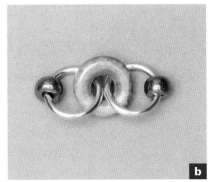

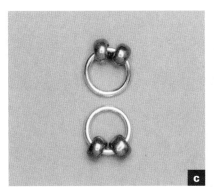

Prep: Open all of the rings.

1. Add a glass ring and a bead to a large ring. Close the ring **(a)**.

2. Weave a large ring through the same glass ring and also add a bead. Close the ring. Set this section aside for a moment **(b)**.

3. Add two beads to a large ring and close the ring. Repeat so that you have two large rings with two beads on each ring **(c)**.

color option

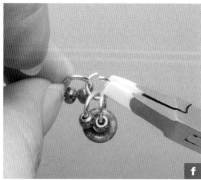

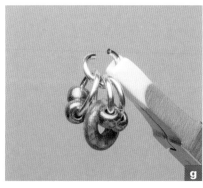

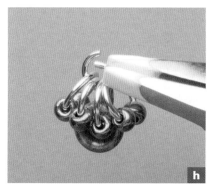

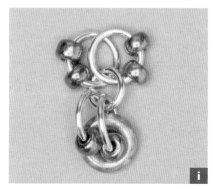

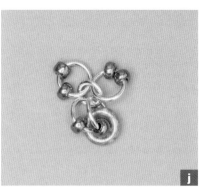

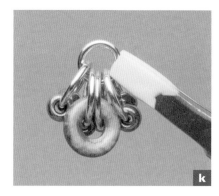

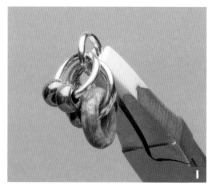

4. Grasp your piece from steps 1 and 2 and weave a medium ring through both the jump rings. Make sure both beads fall to the same side of the glass ring. Don't close it yet **(d)**.

5. Add both large rings with beads from step 3 to the open ring. Close the ring **(e–h)**.

6. Lay the piece flat and adjust or flip the large rings with beads open away from each other—like pages of a book. These large rings with beads should not be layered on top of each other **(i, j)**.

7. Grab the medium ring from the center of the piece with your pliers and lift it off the flat surface. When viewing it from the side, ensure that all the beads are on the same side of the glass ring. You may need to push the beads to the correct side with your fingers **(k, l)**.

8. Carefully use a slightly bent wire piece to weave through only the two large rings with beads. This wire mostly follows the same path of the medium ring, but only goes through the

two large rings at the top. This wire marks the path of the next ring **(m, n)**.

9. Weave a tiny clasp ring in the path marked by the wire. Also add the earring wire before closing. Close the ring **(o, p)**.

10. Notice the "eye" where just two (not all four large rings) large rings intersect when viewing the earring from the side. The wire indicates the path of the next tiny ring. This tiny ring is woven here to prevent the beads from moving toward the front of the earring **(q)**.

11. Weave the tiny ring in the "eye." Close the ring. Notice it is in alignment with the medium ring **(r)**.

12. Repeat step 11 on the opposite side of the earring. If you lay the earring flat, you can more clearly see the tiny rings in their proper position **(s)**.

13. You're done! The earrings may flatten when stored, but as soon as you lift them by the earring wire, they pop back into their caterpillar shape **(t)**.

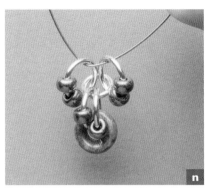

m

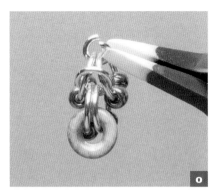

n

o

p

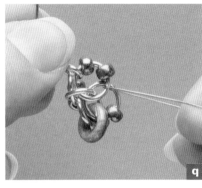

q

r

s

t

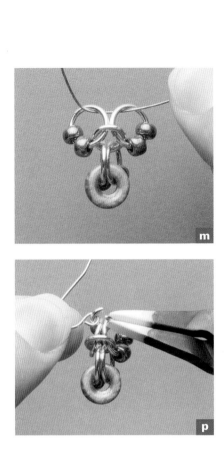

color options

japanese rubber bloom earrings

Shiny, brightly colored enameled copper jump rings join forces with delicate rubber rings to create these blooming flower earrings. This a fun, reversible-color variation of the Japanese Flower weave. Once you get the hang of the pattern, you can create pendants, bracelets, and more.

REFERENCE	METAL/TYPE	QTY	RING SIZE	RING GAUGE		AR
				SWG	MM	
medium ring, color 1	enameled copper, peacock blue	14	3/16 in. (4.8mm)	19	1	4.7
medium ring, color 2	enameled copper, black	14	3/16 in. (4.8mm)	19	1	4.7
rubber ring	silicone rubber, green	52	7/64 in. (2.8mm)	19	1	2.8
tiny clasp ring	enameled copper, black	4	1/8 in. (3.2mm)	20	.8	4.4
pair of black niobium earring wires						

Tools: 2 pairs of flatnose pliers with thin jaws
Length of Time: 1 1/2 hours or less

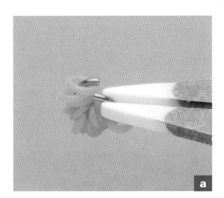

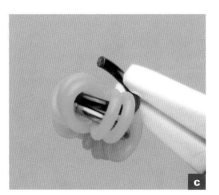

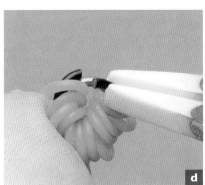

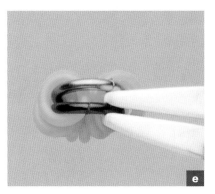

Prep: Open all of the rings.

1. Add 12 rubber rings to a medium color 1 ring. Close the ring. You will need to smoosh the rubber rings down with your pliers to find room to close the ring **(a, b)**.

2. Weave a medium color 2 ring through all 12 of the rubber rings so the two colored rings lay on top of each other. Close the ring. You will have to push it through firmly and make sure it goes through each rubber ring. Smoosh the rubber rings down with your pliers to close the ring **(c–e)**.

tip The tiny rubber rings are quite delicate and should not be stretched or they may break. To make a bracelet, connect each flower with jump rings—NOT with the tiny rubber rings.

design option

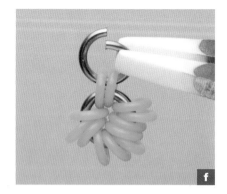

f

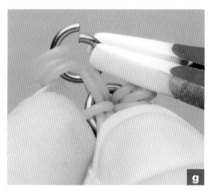

g

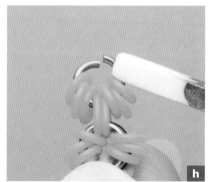

h

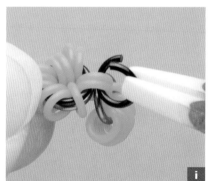

i

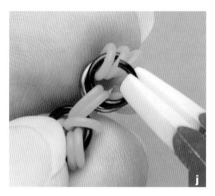

j

k

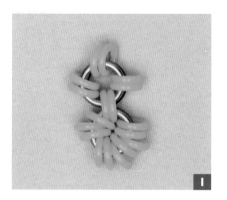

l

color option

3. Weave a medium color 1 ring through any two rubber rings. Before closing it, add six rubber rings **(f–h)**. Close the ring.

4. As in step 2, weave a medium color 2 ring through the same path as the previous ring. It will start going through two from the center unit and then continue weaving through the six rubber rings. When you weave this ring, make sure it is on the same side as the first color 2 ring from step 2 **(i–k)**.

5. Put the piece on a flat surface and separate out the six rubber rings into three pairs as shown. You have created the first "arm" from the center of the unit. In the following steps, you will create five additional arms from the center. Each arm will also be connected to each other **(l)**.

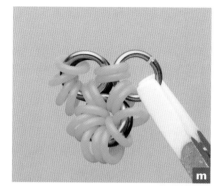

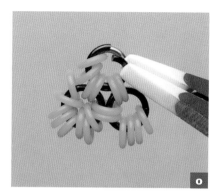

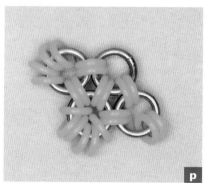

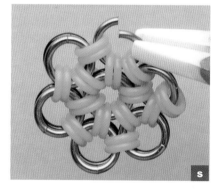

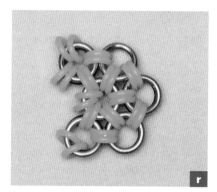

design option

6. Weave a medium color 1 ring through the next two rubber rings from the center of the unit and also weave through the closest pair of rubber rings you separated out in the previous step. Before closing, add two rubber rings. Close the ring **(m, n)**.

7. As in step 4, weave a medium color 2 ring, following the same path as the ring you just closed in the previous step. Make sure it is on the color 2 side of the unit **(o)**.

8. Continue working your way around the center unit, repeating steps 6 and 7 until you reach the first "arm" **(p–r)**.

9. When you reach the first "arm," simply scoop up the remaining rubber rings **(s)**. Before closing, add two rubber rings. Finish your earrings by connecting two tiny clasp rings to the final rubber rings **(t)** and to the earring wire.

10. Weave a color 2 ring in the same path. Close the ring.

buoyant promenade necklace

Floating glass rings sit in perfect position, creating a scalloped look. This graceful necklace demonstrates another style of Japanese weaving techniques. Take extra care when working with these enameled copper rings, as they can become distorted quite easily. It's best to reduce the amount of overlap when trying to close them. Instead, push and scrape the ends together for great closures.

You will need...

REFERENCE	METAL/TYPE	QTY	RING SIZE	RING GAUGE		AR
				SWG	MM	
large ring	aluminum	30	3/8 in. (9.5mm)	14	2	5.1
medium ring	enameled copper, red	60	3/16 in. (4.8mm)	19	1	4.7
glass ring	Czech glass, light red	30	9.5mm OD	—	—	1.5
tiny ring	enameled copper, red	60	1/8 in. (3.2mm)	20	0.8	4.4
medium clasp ring	aluminum	1	3/16 in. (4.8mm)	18	1.2	4.1
tiny clasp ring	aluminum	2	1/8 in. (3.2mm)	18	1.2	2.8
rhodium-plated lobster claw clasp						

Tools: 2 pairs of flatnose pliers and heavy-duty pliers for handling 14-gauge aluminum
Length of Time: 3 hours or less

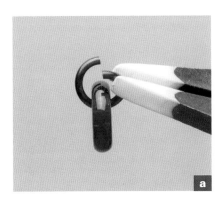
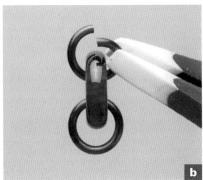
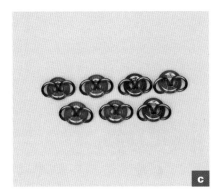

Prep: Open all of the rings.

1. Add a glass ring to a medium ring. Close the ring **(a)**.
2. Weave a second medium ring through the same glass ring. Close the ring **(b)**.
3. Repeat steps 1 and 2 to create multiple glass ring units. You will need approximately 30 units for an 18" necklace **(c)**.

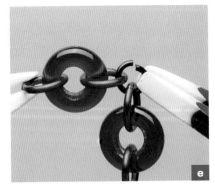

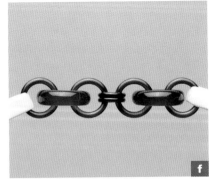

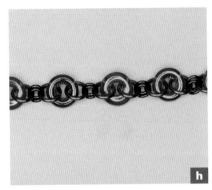

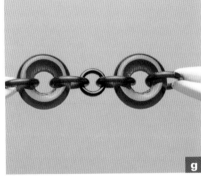

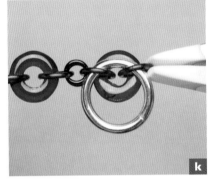

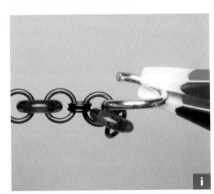

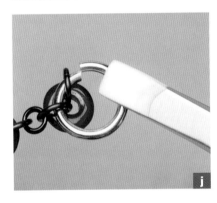

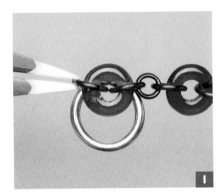

4. Weave a tiny ring through one of the medium rings from a glass ring unit. Before closing, also weave through a single medium ring from another glass ring unit, connecting them together **(d, e)**. Close the ring.

5. Weave a second tiny ring in the same exact path as in step 4. Close the ring **(f, g)**.

6. Repeat steps 4 and 5 until you reach the desired length **(h)**.

7. Switch to heavy-duty pliers. Weave a large ring through the last two medium rings. This ring is woven into the same exact position as the glass ring **(i–l)**.

8. Weave a large ring through the next two medium rings on the same side of the glass as the first large ring **(n–q)**.

9. Repeat step 8 until there are no more medium rings **(r, s)**.

10. Attach the lobster claw clasp by using a tiny clasp ring to connect the medium ring to the clasp **(t)**.

11. On the opposite end, you can either remove the tiny enameled copper rings or keep them for a bit of added length. Add a tiny clasp ring and then a medium clasp ring to this end **(u)**.

tip Notice the large ring fills in the space within the medium rings and also pushes the tiny rings slightly forward. In the following steps, make sure that each large ring is woven on the same side of the glass. This will allow all the glass rings to look the same as they will be in front of the large ring when viewing the necklace from the front **(m)**.

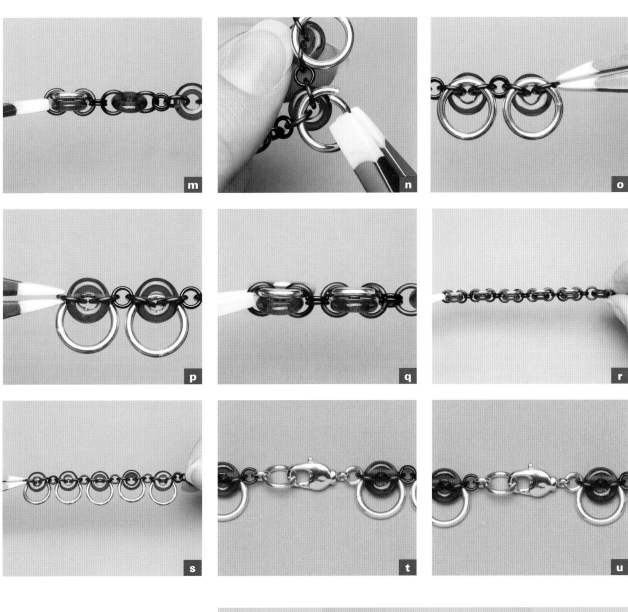

fold & gather linear star pendant

Brightly colored rubber rings are pulled through each other and then folded and stacked to form this striped pendant. Joining the loose rubber ends create star-shaped points. The pendant measures 1¾".

REFERENCE	METAL/TYPE	QTY	RING SIZE	RING GAUGE		AR
				SWG	MM	
extra-large ring	aluminum	1	1/2 in. (12.7mm)	16	1.6	8.9
large ring, color 1	silicone rubber, pink	12	5/16 in. (7.9mm)	16*	1.6	4.3
large ring, color 2	silicone rubber, purple	12	5/16 in. (7.9mm)	16*	1.6	4.3
small ring	silicone rubber, black	12	1/8 in. (3.2mm)	14	2	1.5
medium ring	aluminum	6	3/16 in. (4.8mm)	16	1.2	3.2
medium clasp ring	aluminum	1	3/16 in. (4.8mm)	18	1.2	4.1
tiny clasp ring	aluminum	4	1/8 in. (3.2mm)	18	1.2	2.8

aluminum chain, desired length, and rhodium-plated swivel lobster claw clasp

If you can't find 16-gauge 5/16-in. rubber rings, you may substitute 14-gauge rubber.

Tools: 1 pair of roundnose, chainnose, or bentnose pliers, 2 pairs of flatnose pliers, and 2 pairs of heavy-duty pliers
Length of Time: 2 hours or less

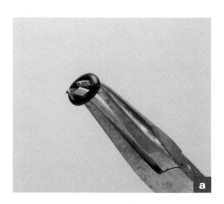
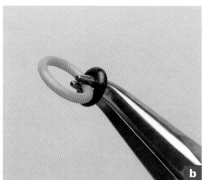
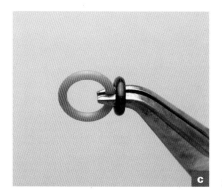

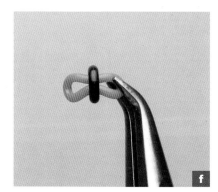

Prep: Open the medium, medium clasp, and tiny clasp rings.

1. Using the roundnose, chainnose, or bentnose pliers, pry open a small rubber ring **(a)**.
2. Very gently grasp a color 1 large rubber ring and pull it halfway through the small rubber ring **(b–f)**.

tip Roundnose pliers can pinch the rubber rings if too much pressure is used. Ensure you use a very gentle grip and only apply minimum pressure on the rubber rings. It works really well to slightly begin to pull it through and then quickly insert one tip of the plier in the rubber ring and then continue to pull through the large rubber ring.

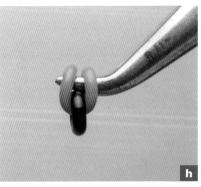

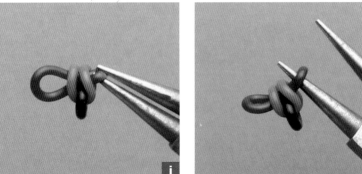

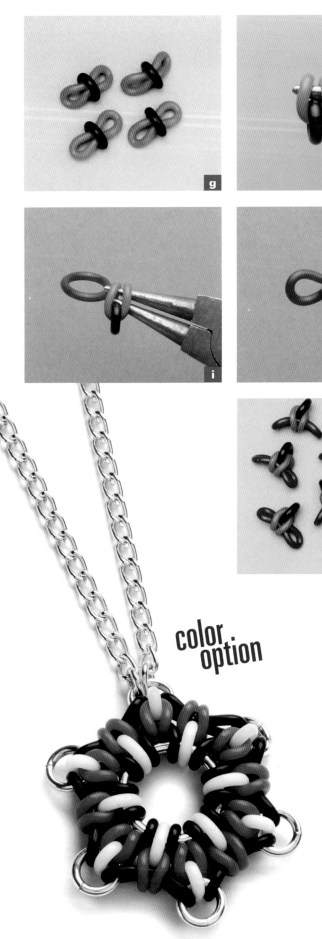

color option

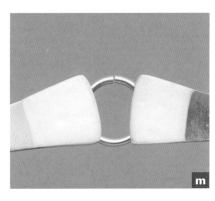

3. Repeat steps 1 and 2 to create 10 total units **(g)**.

4. Fold the large color 1 ring and insert both tips of the pliers inside the folded rubber ring **(h)**.

5. Gently pry open the color 1 large ring and gently pull through the color 2 large ring **(i–k)**.

6. Repeat steps 4 and 5 with the remaining nine units **(l)**.

7. Use flatnose pliers to open the extra-large ring **(m)**.

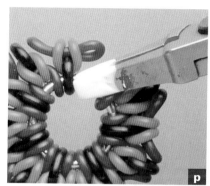

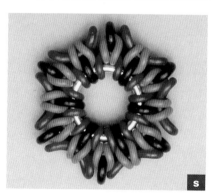

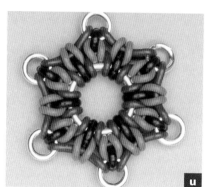

8. Fold the color 2 large ring and slide it on the extra-large ring **(n)**.

9. Slide on another rubber ring unit through the small rubber ring, exactly opposite of step 8 **(o)**.

10. Repeat steps 8 and 9 with the remaining rubber units **(p)**.

11. Close the extra-large ring. You will need to smoosh down the rubber units with your fingers and the pliers in order to find enough room to close it **(q–s)**. Strong but smaller pliers are very helpful here.

12. Weave a medium ring through three adjacent loops to create a single point. Close the ring **(t)**.

13. Repeat step 12 with the remaining five points **(u)**.

14. Add a tiny clasp ring to each end of the pre-made chain and also weave each through a medium ring of any point of the star pendant.

15. Refer to the "Finishing a pre-made chain" section on p. 15 to add a lobster claw clasp.

celtic diamond pendant

This stunning Celtic weave variation forms a distinctive diamond shape that incorporates shiny glass rings and beads. This is a tricky pattern to master, as slight changes in the glass ring thicknesses can affect this weave greatly. This pendant measures 1¾" square.

You will need...

REFERENCE	METAL/TYPE	QTY	RING SIZE	RING GAUGE		AR
				SWG	MM	
large ring	aluminum	12	3/8 in. (9.5mm)*	16	1.6	6.5
medium ring	aluminum	12	1/4 in. (6.4mm)	18	1.2	5.7
small ring	aluminum	8–12	5/32 in. (4mm)	18	1.2	3.6
glass ring	Czech glass, light cobalt	4	9.5mm OD**	—	—	1.5
bead	6º seed beads, Miyuki, cobalt	8	—	—	—	—
medium clasp ring	aluminum	1	3/16 in. (4.8mm)	18	1.2	4.1
tiny clasp ring	aluminum	2	1/8 in. (3.2mm)	18	1.2	2.8

aluminum chain, desired length, and rhodium-plated swivel lobster-claw clasp

Depending on the thickness of the glass ring, this large jump ring size may need to increase 1/64" or more. Try ring size 25/64" (9.9mm) or 13/32" (10.3mm).
**Thin 9.0mm glass rings tend not to work at all for this pattern. Thicker glass rings may require adjustments with the large jump ring size.*

Tools: 2 pairs of flatnose pliers plus 2 pairs of large pliers
Length of Time: 2 hours or less

Prep: Close eight large rings. Open all of the other rings.

1. Create a chain of four glass rings and three large rings **(a)**.

2. Weave a large ring through the final glass ring. Before closing, bring the opposite end toward the open ring and slide on the first glass ring. Lay the entire piece flat to ensure that the weave does not twist while joining the two ends. Close the ring **(b–d)**.

3. Encircle the top-most glass ring by laying a large closed ring over it **(e)**.

4. With a large closed ring, encircle the same glass ring underneath the weave so that both large rings now sandwich this top portion of the weave **(f)**.

5. Switch to the narrower pliers. Weave a medium ring down through the "eye" indicated, scooping up all three large rings. Before closing, add a bead. Close the ring **(g–i)**. (This is nearly the same path as in the "Celtic Crossroads Bracelet," p. 46).

If you lift up the entire weave when weaving this medium ring, the large rings will move out of position and you will no longer see the "eye." To return the weave back to the proper position, lay the whole piece flat again and pull out the two large rings away from the rest of the weave. Gently re-position the large rings by flipping one down over the top glass ring and the second large ring should be flipped under the weave encircling the same glass ring. Alternatively, you can leave the whole weave flat and carefully weave in the medium ring so that you don't need to reposition the large rings.

6. Repeat step 5 through the "eye" directly adjacent to the previous "eye," which is hovering over the same glass ring. The large rings will hold their position a bit better while you weave in this ring. Try to press the two large rings together while weaving in the medium ring so that they don't flop around **(j–n)**.

We will now be weaving in only one medium ring into a slanted position that will lock the large rings into place. Carefully read the next few steps, as the position of this ring and the way it is woven into place is different to what was done in previous steps.

7. Weave a medium ring in through the "eye" directly below the first "eye" and below the glass ring from step 5. The easiest way to weave this ring is by inserting it through the center of the entire weave and coming up from behind and through the large ring at the back of the weave. Do not close it yet **(o–q)**.

8. Change the position of your hand and pliers to grasp the ring from the opposite side of the ring. This changes the direction of the hook, which is necessary in the next step. Do not close it yet **(r)**.

9. Push the ring underneath and through the single large ring to the left of the sandwiched rings. It should look like it is slanted down toward the left. Close the ring **(s, t)**.

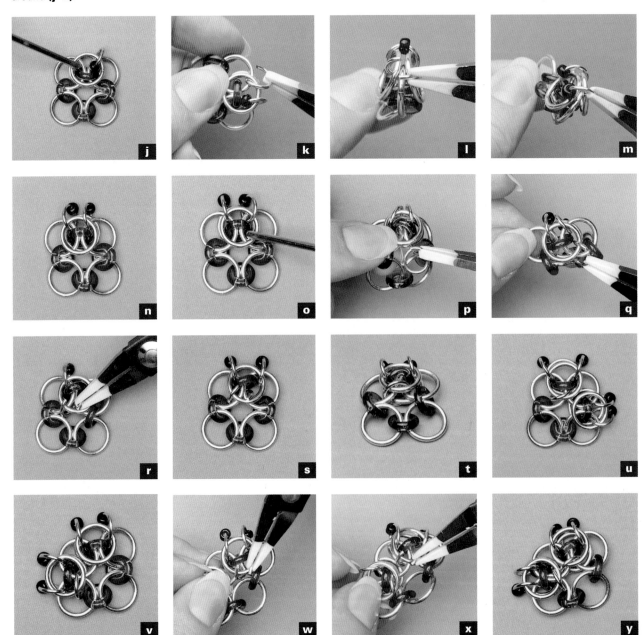

10. Repeat steps 3–6 with medium rings and beads while rotating the weave counter-clockwise so that you can see the glass ring you are working with at the top **(u)**. **Photo v** shows the piece turned counterclockwise.

11. Repeat steps 7–9 with a medium ring **(w–y)**.

12. Repeat steps 3–9 to complete the final two sections. Make sure you continue to work in the same direction so all of the medium slanted rings in the center all angle in the same direction **(z, aa)**.

tip

As the pendant is still loose during these next few steps, the center slanted rings may move out of position. Push these center medium rings back down to the center of the pendant to keep the angled position.

13. Weave a small ring through the two medium rings at the top of the weave. Make sure before closing this ring that both beads are on the same side. Close the ring **(bb)**.

14. Weave a second small ring in front of the previous one and before closing, push it down and through the previous small ring, allowing the two rings to cross paths **(cc, dd)**. This is the same mobiusing technique used in the "Synthesis Necklace," p. 25.

15. Repeat steps 15 and 16 with the remaining medium rings, making sure to push the beads over to the same side **(ee, ff)**.

16. Feel your pendant and try to slightly bend it at the center. If the center slanted rings move out of the proper position, then the pendant is not firm enough yet. An additional small ring should be added and mobiused to at least two tips to make the pendant firmer. If needed add the additional small rings to two tips that are opposite of each other to make the pendant look more balanced. If it still feels a bit loose, add an additional ring to a third tip. Finally, check it once more and if needed, add a final ring to the fourth tip. Double-check that the center slanted rings are still in the proper position as you

are adding these final small rings. The glass rings each vary slightly in thickness (gauge), which is why for this pattern, we have to make adjustments to ensure the pendant keeps its proper shape. This is the same reason why the thinner small glass rings do not work well for this weave with these exact ring sizes **(gg–hh)**.

17. Weave a small ring through a mobiused tip and close the ring in order to attach a chain to it. (See photo of finished project on p. 66.)

18. Weave tiny clasp rings connecting the chain to the small ring. Refer to the "Finishing a pre-made chain" section, p. 15, to add a lobster claw clasp.

crosscut bracelet

Two decorative strips of sparkling glass rings and beads intersect in a slightly zig-zag formation in this stylish bracelet. This pattern uses techniques from the Japanese style of weaving.

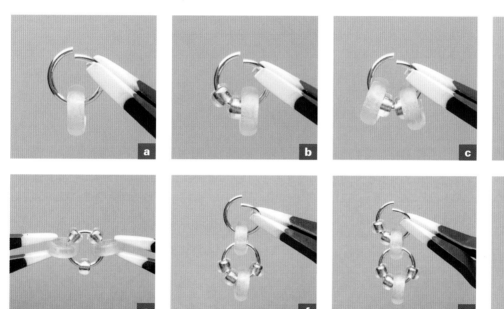

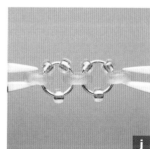

Prep: Open all of the rings.

1. Add a glass ring to a large ring. Don't close the ring yet **(a)**.
2. To the same large ring, add two beads, then another glass ring and finally one more bead. Close the ring **(b–e)**.
3. Weave a large ring through the right-most glass ring. Don't close it yet **(f)**.
4. As in step 2, add two beads, a glass ring, and finally one more bead. Close the ring **(g–j)**.
5. Repeat steps 3 and 4 until you reach the desired length.

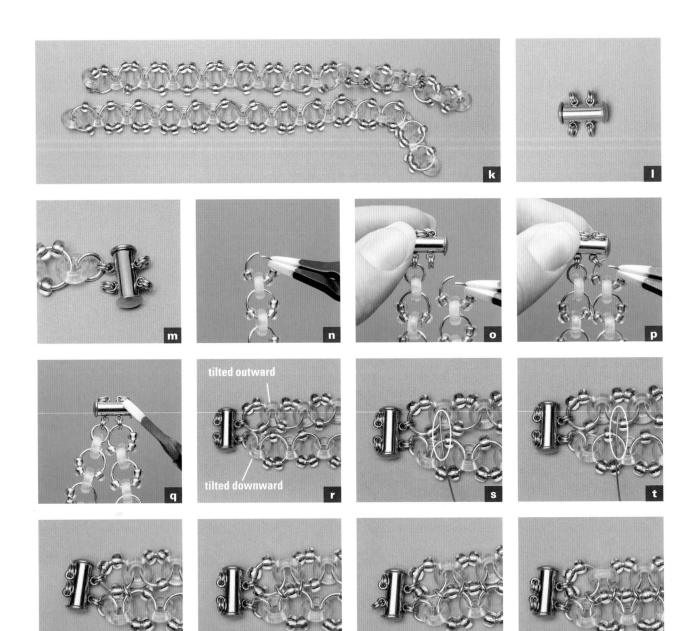

6. Repeat steps 3–5 to complete another strip the exact same length **(k)**.

7. Prepare the slide clasp by adding two tiny clasp rings to each loop of the clasp. In the following steps, you will connect the clasp to the two strips for stability before joining the strips together **(l)**.

8. Take one of the strips and weave a medium clasp ring through the final glass ring; also weave through two tiny clasp rings. Close the ring **(m)**.

9. Grab the second strip and weave a large ring through a glass ring at one end. Also add three beads. Don't close it yet **(n)**.

10. Line up this strip to the other strip already attached to the clasp. Make sure the single beads are facing each other in the middle of both strips. Weave through the tiny clasp rings **(o, p)**, and then close the ring.

tip The clasp point has to end in this off-set manner so the zig-zag path will work in the following steps.

11. Lay the bracelet flat and push the first two glass rings from each strip closer together in the center of the bracelet. The glass rings should be creating a V-shape and face away from each other. When you add the tiny rings in the following steps, the glass rings will no longer hold the V-shape. That is just the nature of this pattern **(r)**.

12. In the following steps, the tiny rings will join the two strips, creating a zig-zag path, which traps a single bead in between each tiny ring. The piece of wire in **photo s** indicates where the first tiny ring will be woven to connect the two strips. The piece of wire in **photo t** indicates where

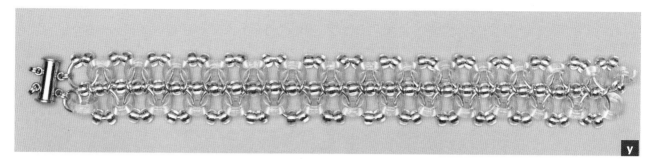

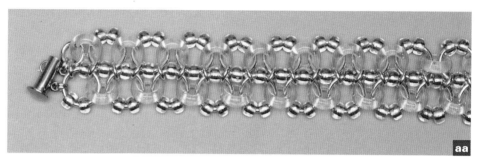

the second tiny ring will be woven. When adding these tiny rings, a single bead should fall to each side of the closed ring **(s, t)**.

13. Weave a tiny ring connecting the two strips as shown in the photo. Close the ring **(u)**.

14. Weave a tiny ring connecting the two strips as shown in the photo. Close the ring **(v)**.

15. Repeat steps 13 and 14 down the length of the piece **(w–y)**.

16. End your bracelet the same way you began. Each strip will end the opposite way that it started to finish the zig-zag path correctly. Add a tiny ring joining the medium clasp ring to the large ring on each end **(z, aa)**.

color
option

interwoven network bracelet

This reversible-color rubber cuff measures almost 2" wide. Thick rings are used to connect the rubber and also provide strength. There is no clasp needed! This pattern uses techniques from the Japanese style of weaving. Depending on the length needed, the way the bracelet closes on itself may vary.

You will need...

REFERENCE	METAL/TYPE	QTY	RING SIZE	RING GAUGE		AR
				SWG	MM	
large rubber, color 1	silicone rubber, black	23–25	25/64 in. (9.9mm)	14	2	5.4
large rubber, color 2	silicone rubber, white	23–25	25/64 in. (9.9mm)	14	2	5.4
medium rubber, color 1	silicone rubber, black	8–15	15/64 in. (6mm)	14	2	3
medium rubber, color 2	silicone rubber, white	8–15	15/64 in. (6mm)	14	2	3
small rubber	silicone rubber, black	16–20	1/8 in. (3.2mm)	14	2	1.7
small ring	aluminum	84–94	3/16 in. (4.8mm)	16	1.6	3.2

Tools: 1 pair of bentnose, chainnose, or roundnose pliers for pulling the rubber through and 2 pairs of flatnose made for handling 16-gauge wire.
Length of Time: 2 1/2 hours or less

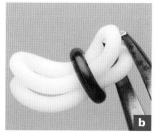

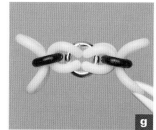

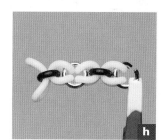

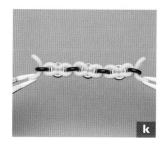

Prep: Open all of the rings.

1. Slide a small rubber ring onto the chainnose, bentnose, or roundnose pliers, and then grasp two large color B rubber rings inside the pliers **(a)**.

2. Roll the small rubber ring to the center of the two large rubber rings **(b, c)**.

3. Repeat steps 1 and 2 to create multiple rubber ring units. You'll need approximately 20 for an 8" bracelet **(d)**.

4. Fold one rubber ring from the unit and weave a small ring through both loops. Before closing, add a folded rubber ring from another unit. Close the ring **(e–g)**.

5. Continue to create a short chain of four rubber ring units and three small rings **(h–k)**.

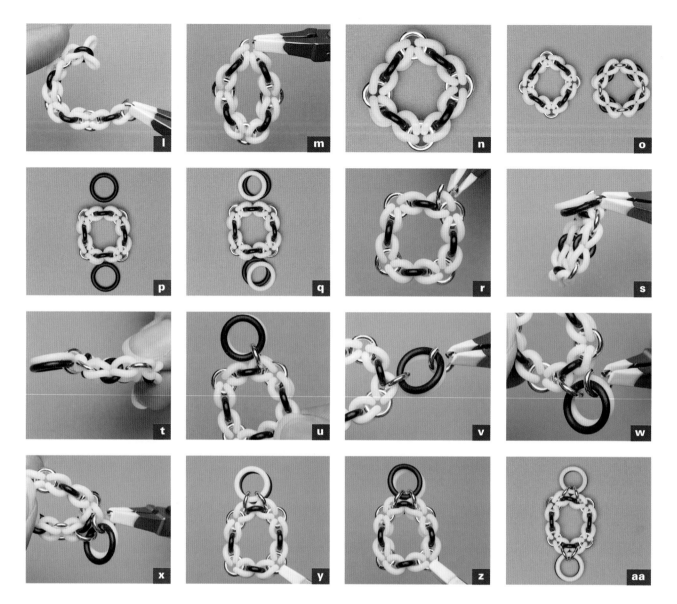

6. Bring the ends of your chain together and connect them with a small ring to make a square-shaped piece. Make sure the chain does not twist as you join the ends **(l, m)**.

7. Create multiple square units like this by repeating steps 4–6. You will need about 5 square units for 8" of length **(n)**.

tip

Be careful not to accidentally roll the square unit as in the second unit in the photo. You want the small jump rings to remain parallel to your work surface **(o)**.

8. To start the reversible pattern, two large rubber rings, one of each color will be added to the square unit. **Photos p** and **q** show where they will be added (between two corners).

9. Weave a small ring through the large rubber ring from your square unit, just above the small rubber ring. Before closing, slide on two large rubber rings (one of each color). Close the ring **(r–u)**.

10. Weave a small ring through the two large rings you added, and continue down through the large ring directly adjacent to the one you just wove through. Close the ring. Each small ring should sit above the small rubber ring. Alternatively, you can weave through the large ring from your square piece first and then through the two large rings **(v–z)**.

11. Repeat steps 9 and 10 directly across on the opposite side of the square unit. Make sure your large color A and color B rings are on the same side of the entire unit **(aa, bb)**.

12. Repeat steps 9–11 with the remaining two sides of the square unit. Alternatively you can add the large rings by weaving in a clockwise or counter-clockwise direction. I find it easiest to continue to see the square shape by weaving opposite ends first **(cc, dd)**.

13. Pairs of medium color A and color B rubber rings, following the same reversible pattern, will be added in between only two sets of the large pairs of rings. These medium rings will be added on opposite sides. **Photo ee** shows where these rings will be added.

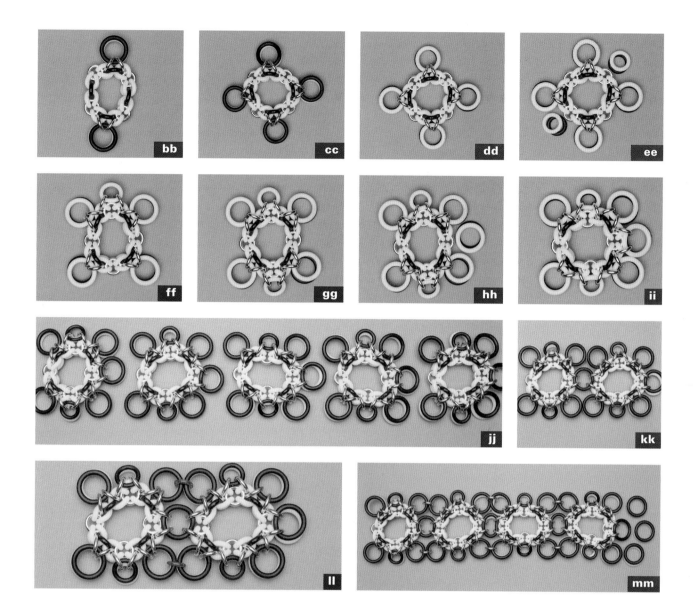

14. Connect the medium rubber ring pairs to your square unit by weaving through the large rubber rings and above the initial corners of the square unit from step 7 (see **photo n**). It is normal for the medium rubber rings to slightly flatten out along the bottom due to the way they are stretched **(ff, gg)**.

15. On only one open side, connect two large rubber rings (one of each color) in the same way you connected the medium rubber rings in step 14 **(hh, ii)**.

16. Repeat steps 9–14 to create four or five pieces **(jj)**.

17. Connect the center pair of large rubber rings to the next unit, filling in the blank space **(kk)**.

18. Also connect the top and bottom sets of rings to each other **(ll)**.

19. If adding an entire additional unit will make the bracelet too long, simply add three pairs of large rubber rings. These will connect directly to the final three pairs and also to the opposite end of your bracelet to close it on itself **(mm)**.

encapsulated delicacy bracelet

This project introduces a fresh take on a well-known weave named Byzantine. This is a variation of a Byzantine variation called X-Lock Byzantine, which features large and small glass rings and beads. A stately bracelet comes together rather quickly.

REFERENCE	METAL/TYPE	QTY	RING SIZE	RING GAUGE		AR
				SWG	MM	
large ring	aluminum	28	21/64 in. (8.3mm)	18	1.2	9.1
medium ring	aluminum	28	1/4 in. (6.4mm)	18	1.2	5.7
large glass ring	Czech glass, chrysoprase	7–9	14mm OD	—	—	2.2
small glass ring	Czech glass, smoke	7–9	9–9.5mm OD	—	—	1.5–1.8
bead	6º seed beads, Miyuki, Picasso opaque dark teal	24–30	—	—	—	—
medium clasp ring	aluminum	4	7/32 in. (5.6mm)	18	1.2	7.4
tiny clasp ring	aluminum	4	1/8 in. (3.2mm)	18	1.2	2.8

rhodium-plated renaissance toggle clasp

Tools: 2 pairs of flatnose pliers
Length of Time: 2 hours or less

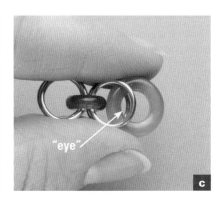

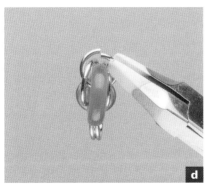

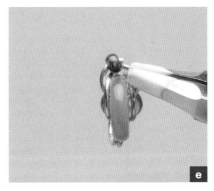

Prep: Open all of the rings.

1. Weave four large rings though a small glass ring. Close each ring **(a)**.

2. Repeat step 1 with the remaining small glass rings. You'll need about seven glass ring units for an 8" bracelet **(b)**.

3. Separate the large rings into two pairs and place the large glass ring in between one of the pairs of rings **(c)**.

4. Weave a medium ring though the small "eye" created in between the pair of large rings and the large glass ring. Don't close the ring yet **(d)**.

5. Add a bead to the medium ring and now close it **(e)**. You can place your pliers below the bead on one side in order to get a better grip on the ring and obtain a proper closure **(f, g)**.

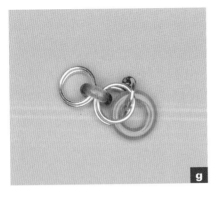

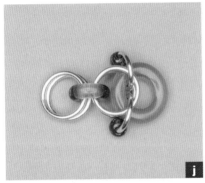

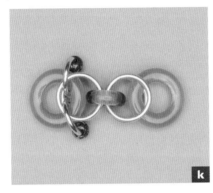

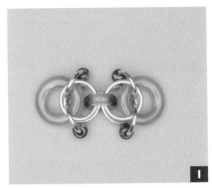

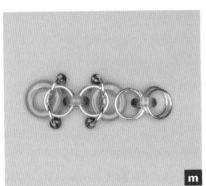

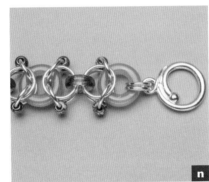

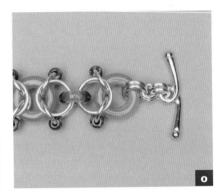

tip It may be tricky to weave the medium rings through the "eye." Try to change the direction from which you enter the ring. You can also try weaving through just one large jump ring and the glass ring and then gently dig through to the other side to weave through the second large jump ring (**h, i**).

6. Repeat steps 5 and 6 on the opposite side of the same pair of large rings. Two medium rings with a bead have now been woven through the same "eye" (**j**).

7. Rotate the weave and line up a new large glass ring in between the second pair of large rings from the same small glass ring unit (**k**).

8. Repeat steps 4–6. Notice that the medium rings with beads naturally face each other (**l**).

9. To complete your bracelet, continue to connect small glass ring units to large glass rings (**m**).

10. Attach the loop half of your toggle by connecting it to two medium clasp rings through the final large glass ring (**n**).

11. At the opposite end, add two medium clasp rings to the final large ring. Also add two pairs of tiny rings and the bar half of the toggle (**o**).

12. You can add a smaller bit of length at the end without adding a whole other unit by simply connecting a small glass ring to the final large glass ring using two medium rings (not a medium clasp ring). Then finish adding the toggle using the medium clasp rings (**p**).

into orbit necklace

This statement necklace features steel donuts and very large glass rings. The steel donuts are suspended inside of the large black glass triangular units. This necklace showcases six completed triangular units.

| REFERENCE | METAL/TYPE | QTY | RING SIZE | RING GAUGE | | AR |
				SWG	MM	
large ring	anodized aluminum	3–21	5/16 in. (7.9mm)	16	1.6	5.4
medium ring	anodized aluminum	11–40	1/4 in. (6.4mm)	16	1.6	4.2
extra-large glass ring	Czech glass, black	4–16	17.7mm OD	—	—	2.85
steel ring	stainless steel donut	6–14	12.1mm OD	—	—	1.78

large gunmetal-plated spring-trigger clasp

Tools: 2 pairs of flatnose pliers
Length of Time: 2 1/2 hours or less

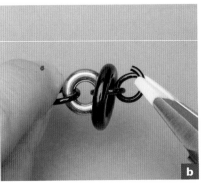

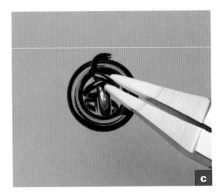

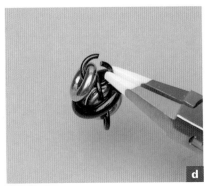

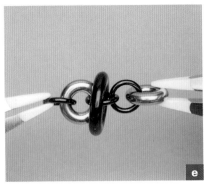

Prep: Open all of the rings.

1. Weave two medium rings through a steel donut. Close each ring **(a)**. Repeat to create a total of 4–6 units.

2. Rest an extra-large glass ring on the steel donut by weaving a medium ring through a medium ring from the unit. Don't close it yet **(b, c)**.

3. Add a steel ring. Close the ring **(d, e)**.

4. Repeat steps 2–4 on the opposite end of the steel ring from step 1 **(f)**.

5. Connect the two extra-large glass rings above the center steel donut with a large ring. Close the ring. This is one completed unit **(g, h)**.

6. Weave a medium ring through a steel ring on one end **(i)**. Do not close it yet.

7. Rest an extra-large glass ring on top of the same steel ring by pushing the open medium jump ring through the glass ring hole. Don't close it still **(j)**.

8. Add a unit from step 1 onto your open ring that has pushed through the glass ring. Move the glass ring over to find room to close the ring. Now close the ring **(k–m)**.

9. Rest an extra large ring on the steel donut on the end by slightly pushing it through the glass **(n, o)**.

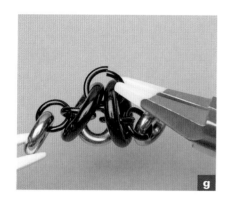

g

h

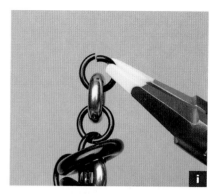

i

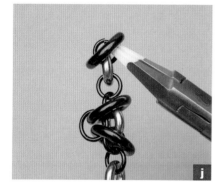

j

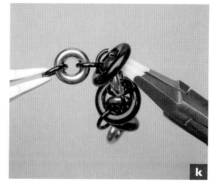

k

l

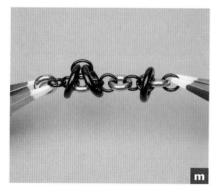

m

n

o

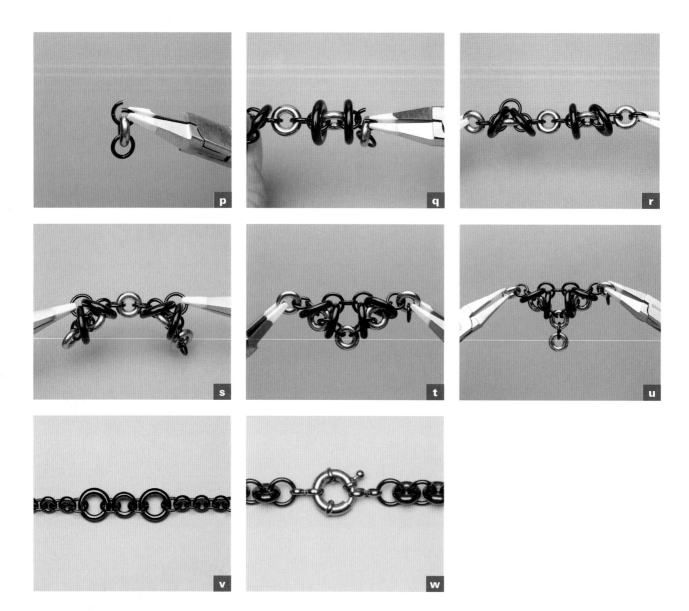

10. Open the medium ring from another steel ring unit and attach it to the medium ring you pushed through in the previous step **(p–r)**.

11. Connect the two extra-large glass rings with a large ring as in step 5 **(s)**.

12. Connect the two completed triangular units together with a medium ring that weaves through both large rings. You now have a more pronounced triangle shape **(t)**.

13. Add a single steel donut to the center steel donut with a large jump ring. The center of your necklace is now complete **(u)**.

14. You can add length a variety of ways including adding more completed triangular units (steps 2–5) or simply adding an assortment of single glass rings of varying sizes to form a pattern you enjoy. The steel donuts are heavy, so make sure you don't add too many steel donuts **(v)**.

15. Add a heavy-duty clasp to help support the weight of this necklace by using medium rings at the clasp point **(w)**.

arctic sphere bracelet

My new favorite weave is Arctic Sphere! The bright blue tones and the spherical shape make this a conversation piece. This requires great dexterity and also being able to use your "pinchers" and even your fingernails, while holding the main parts of the weave steady.

| REFERENCE | METAL/TYPE | QTY | RING SIZE | RING GAUGE | | AR |
				SWG	MM	
extra-large ring	aluminum	16	15/32 in. (11.9mm)	16	1.6	8.4
large ring	aluminum	55	1/4 in. (6.4mm)	18	1.2	5.7
medium ring	enameled copper, peacock blue	32	3/16 in. (4.8mm)	19	1	4.7
glass ring	Czech glass, aqua	8	14mm OD	—	—	2.2
tiny clasp ring	aluminum	4	1/8 in. (3.2mm)	18	1.2	2.8

rhodium-plated craftsman toggle clasp

Tools: 2 pairs of extra-large flatnose pliers
Length of Time: 3 1/2 hours or less

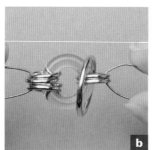
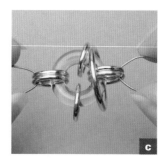
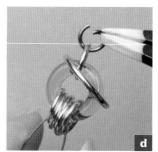

Prep: Open all of the rings.

1. Weave six large rings through a glass ring. Close each ring. Create seven or eight of these units **(a)**.

2. Temporarily separate two large rings from your unit. Rest an extra-large jump ring on the side of glass ring while also encircling the two large rings **(b)**.

3. In the following steps, on each side of the glass ring, one new large ring will be connected to each of the two large rings separated out in the previous step. These pairs of large rings will sandwich both halves of the extra-large ring **(c)**.

4. Return the large rings back to their original position. To create the sandwich, weave a medium ring through a large ring, while ensuring that the extra-large jump ring is still orbiting the glass ring. Don't close it yet **(d)**.

5. Allow a large ring to slide down along the glass and sandwich the extra-large ring. Continue weaving the medium ring through the other half of the sandwich: the large ring **(e, f)**.

6. Create another sandwich with the second half of the extra-large ring **(g–i)**.

tip The two medium rings should sit in opposite directions when viewing it from the side or perpendicular to the glass ring. If the large rings move out of position, you can turn them back up and over the glass ring. Also make sure the medium rings are still opposite of each other and not facing the same direction **(j–q)**.

7. Create a sandwich on the other half of the glass ring, by encircling the glass with an extra-large ring **(r)**.

8. Repeat steps 4–6 to connect the "sandwich" on the other side of this same unit **(s–u)**.

9. Finish this unit by connecting the final hanging large ring and securing the "sandwich" **(v–z)**.

10. Repeat steps 1–9 to create multiple units **(aa)**. You'll need approximately eight for a 7½-in. bracelet.

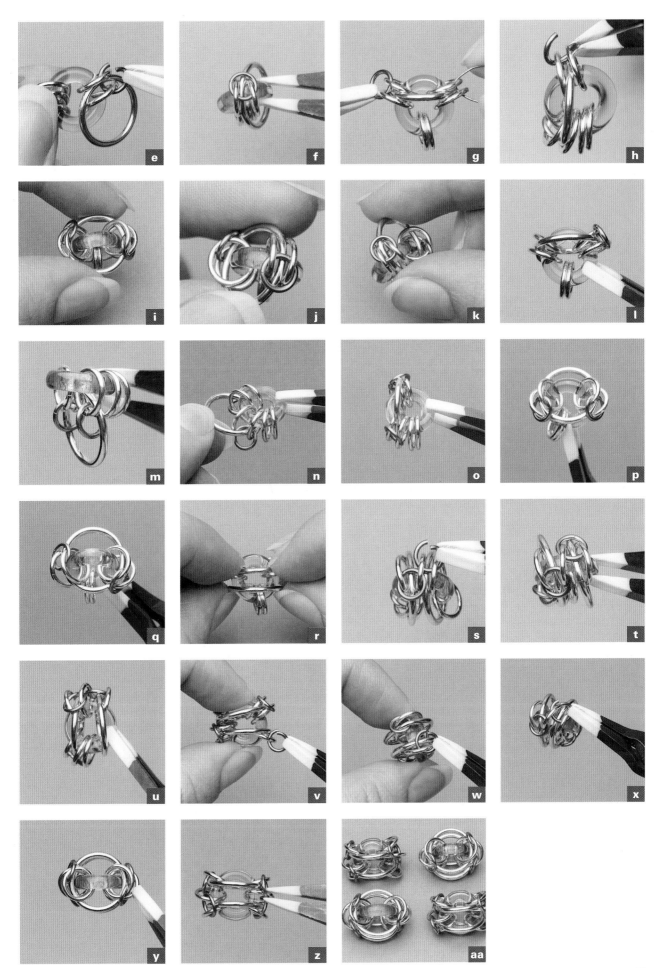

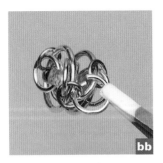
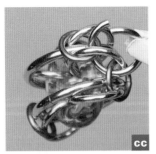
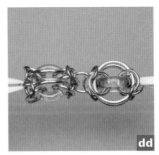

11. Connect each sphere by weaving a large ring diagonally through the medium rings and also up through the center large ring on the side of the sphere **(bb–ee)**.

12. Repeat step 11 and connect all your units. I like to make each unit connect opposite to the previous unit for a staggered effect **(ff)**.

13. Add the toggle loop on one side with a single tiny clasp ring. On the toggle bar, make a three-ring chain of tiny clasp rings that conencts the end to the clasp **(gg)**.

color option

lock & twist bracelet

Twist and fold the rubber into little locked units that connect together to make a two-tone, stretchy bracelet. There is no clasp needed for this piece.

REFERENCE	METAL/TYPE	QTY	RING SIZE	RING GAUGE		AR
				SWG	MM	
rubber ring, color 1	silicone rubber, blue	22	3/8 in. (9.5mm)*	16	1.6	6.5
rubber ring, color 2	silicone rubber, aqua	22	3/8 in. (9.5mm)*	16	1.6	6.5
anodized aluminum ring	anodized aluminum, violet	22	1/4 in. (6.4mm)*	16	1.6	4.2
aluminum ring	aluminum	22	1/4 in. (6.4mm)*	16	1.6	4.2

Tools: 2 pairs of large flatnose pliers
Length of Time: 2 hours or less

* If you can't find rings in these sizes, you may substitute 25/64" (9.9mm) 14-gauge (2mm) rubber rings and 5/16" (7.9mm) 16-gauge (1.6mm) metal rings, as in the pink and gray version on p. 91.

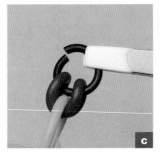
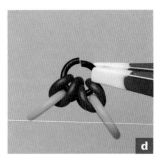

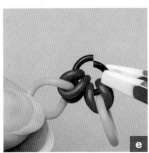

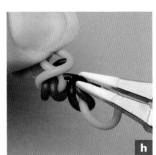

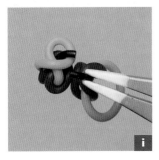
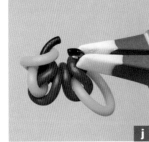
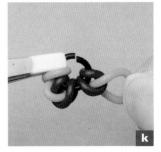
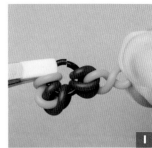

Prep: Open all of the rings.

1. Push a color 1 (blue) rubber ring through a color 2 (aqua) rubber ring **(a)**.

2. Gently grab the entire unit and carefully fold the color 1 ring around the color 2 ring. As you fold it, quickly slide the folded loops onto an anodized aluminum ring (violet). These rubber rings can slip and slide out of place quite easily, so be careful **(b, c)**.

3. Repeat steps 1 and 2, and slide it onto the same anodized aluminum ring. Do not close it yet **(d)**.

4. While still holding the jump ring in your pliers, carefully twist the bottom of the color 2 rubber ring away from your body to form a figure-8 shape **(e–g)**. Continue to push the top loop of the figure 8 on to the hook of the open ring **(h–j)**. Don't close it yet.

5. Change position and hold the ring in the pliers in your non-dominant hand in order to smoosh down the figure 8 you just placed **(k)**.

6. Carefully twist the second color 2 rubber ring away from you to form the figure 8. Slide it on to the hook. Now close the ring **(l–q)**. You now have a unit that reminds me of owl eyes.

7. Weave a second anodized aluminum ring through the entire unit, parallel to the first anodized aluminum ring. Adding another ring firms up this unit and prevents the rubber rings from moving and losing this shape **(r–u)**. Notice the unit has two sides: one that looks more obviously like owl eyes with an angled brow, and one that has a straighter "brow" **(v)**.

8. Repeat steps 1–8 to make multiple units. You will need 11 units for an 8" bracelet **(w)**.

9. Two units will now be connected at the bottom through the color 1 rubber rings with an aluminum ring as shown in **photo x**.

10. Weave an aluminum ring through only the color 1 folded ring sitting at the bottom of a unit. Do not close it yet **(y)**.

11. Weave the aluminum ring through the color 1 rubber rings of a second unit. Make sure the units are facing the same way, with all of the "owl eyes" on one side of the weave **(z–bb)**. Close the ring.

m

n

o

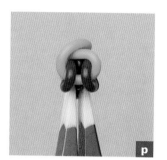
p

q

r

s

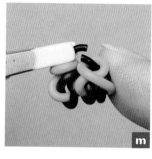
t

owl eyes

u

straight brow
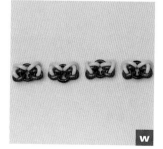
v

w

x

y

z

aa

bb

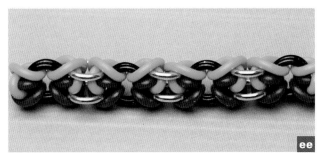

12. These two units will now be connected at the top with a medium ring as shown in **photo cc**.

13. Weave underneath only the color 2 rubber ring at the point where it is twisted. Continue to weave through the other unit going through the same path **(dd)**. Here you are connecting the two twists of the adjoining units, but not actually weaving through the inside of the color 2 rubber rings.

14. Repeat steps 10–13 to complete the desired length and connect the two ends together **(ee)**.

color option

lock & twist pendant

A variation of the bracelet with the same name, this firm and fun pendant features multiple sizes of glass and rubber! There are lots of ring sizes used in this project for the most precise fit. Be careful not to mix up the sizes as you're working.

| REFERENCE | METAL/TYPE | QTY | RING SIZE | RING GAUGE | | AR |
				SWG	MM	
large rubber, color A	silicone rubber, purple	8	25/64 in. (9.9mm)	14	2	5.4
large rubber, color B	silicone rubber, black	8	25/64 in. (9.9mm)	14	2	5.4
glass ring, color A	Czech glass ring, lilac	2	14mm OD	—	—	2.2
glass ring, color B	Czech glass ring, black	1	14mm OD	—	—	2.2
bead, color A	3º seed beads, Toho, purple-lined rainbow	4	—	—	—	—
bead, color B	3º seed beads, Toho, matte black	2	—	—	—	—
giant	aluminum	1	5/8 in. (15.9mm)	14	2	9
extra-large	anodized aluminum, black	4	3/8 in. (9.5mm)	16	1.6	6.5
extra-large	aluminum	2	3/8 in. (9.5mm)	16	1.6	6.5
large	anodized aluminum, black	4	5/16 in. (7.9mm)	16	1.6	5.4
large	aluminum	8	5/16 in. (7.9mm)	16	1.6	5.4
medium	aluminum	10	1/4 in. (6.4mm)	16	1.6	4.2
small	aluminum	8	3/16 in. (4.8mm)	16	1.6	3.2
clasp rings	aluminum	2	7/32 in. (5.6mm)	18	1.2	7.4

Tools: Bentnose, chainnose, or roundnose pliers for pulling the rubber through and flatnose pliers made for handling 16-gauge wire
Length of Time: 2 1/2 hours or less

Note: The step-by-step photos show the pendant made using different ring colors.

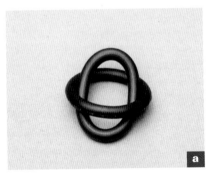

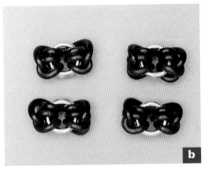

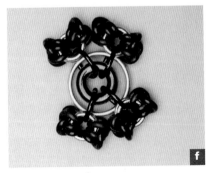

Prep: Close the extra-large ring. Open all other rings.

1. Create four Lock & Twist units as in the "Lock & Twist Bracelet," p. 89, with the large aluminum rings and the two colors of rubber rings **(a, b)**.

2. Place the four units around the giant ring. Place the color B glass ring inside the giant ring **(c)**.

3. Connect each rubber unit to the glass ring and giant ring with a large anodized aluminum ring. This ring is woven through the lower center of the rubber ring unit **(d–f)**.

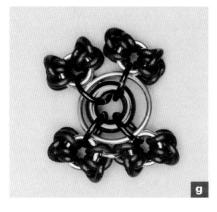

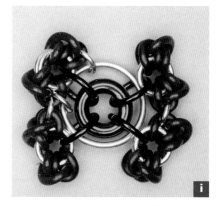

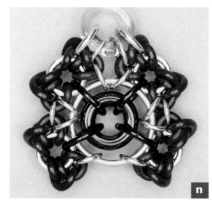

4. Connect two rubber units together with a medium ring that is woven through only the loops of the color A rubber rings **(g)**.

5. Repeat step 4 with the other two rubber units **(h)**.

6. Connect the color A rubber rings to the giant ring by weaving small rings through only the bottom portion of the color A rubber rings **(i, j)**.

7. Add a color A glass ring to the top open section of the pendant. Use a medium ring and weave through the top portion the rubber unit and the glass ring **(k)**.

8. Weave another medium ring on the adjacent side of the glass ring and rubber unit **(l)**.

9. For added stability, weave a medium ring through the bottom loops of the rubber unit and through the glass ring. Repeat on the adjacent side **(m, n)**.

10. Repeat steps 7–9 on the opposite end of the pendant **(o)**.

11. Weave an extra-large ring through the top portion of a single rubber unit. It will look like it is encircling the medium rings inside the unit. Don't close it yet **(p)**.

12. Add a color A bead. Close the ring **(q–s)**.

13. Repeat steps 11 and 12 on the remaining three rubber units **(t)**.

14. Weave an extra-large ring connecting two adjacent rubber ring units. This ring is woven through only the top portion of the rubber units. Add a color B bead, and close the ring **(u, v)**.

15. Repeat step 14 on the opposite side of the pendant.

16. Connect the top glass ring to a pre-made chain using the clasp rings.

17. Finish the pre-made chain by referring to the instructions on p. 15.

lustrous stitched bracelet

An elegant wide cuff gleaming with two colors of glass rings. Many of the rings are added in tight spaces, so patience and great dexterity is helpful. This pattern demonstrates the Japanese style of weaving.

| REFERENCE | METAL/TYPE | QTY | RING SIZE | RING GAUGE | | AR |
				SWG	MM	
large-thick ring	aluminum	13	3/8 in. (9.5mm)	16	1.6	6.5
large-thin ring	aluminum	24	3/8 in. (9.5mm)	18	1.2	8.6
glass ring, color 1	Czech glass, seafoam	92	9.5mm OD	—	—	1.5
glass ring, color 2	Czech glass, clear	26	9.5mm OD	—	—	1.5
bead	6º seed beads, Miyuki, clear	22	—	—	—	—
medium ring	anodized aluminum, champagne	22	1/4 in. (6.4mm)	18	1.2	5.7
small ring	anodized aluminum, champagne	22	3/16 in. (4.8mm)	18	1.2	4.1
tiny ring	anodized aluminum, champagne	36	1/8 in. (3.2mm)	20	0.8	2.8
small clasp ring	aluminum	2	3/16 in. (4.8mm)	18	1.2	4.1
tiny clasp ring	aluminum	6	5/32 in. (4mm)	18	1.2	3.6

rhodium-plated artisan toggle clasp

Tools: 1 pair of large flatnose pliers and 1 pair of small flatnose pliers
Length of Time: 4 hours or less

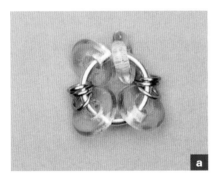

Prep: Close the tiny rings. Open all of the other rings.

1. Start a chain by adding two color 1 glass rings, three tiny rings, two color 1 glass rings, and three more tiny ring on a large-thick ring. Close the ring **(a)**.

2. Weave a large-thick ring through 3 tiny rings from the previous step and add two color 1 glass rings to each side of the ring. Before closing, also add three tiny rings. Close the ring **(b)**.

3. Repeat step 2 for the full desired length **(c)**.

4. We are now going to create a top row using thinner rings. Weave a large-thin ring through one glass ring from the first two adjacent units in your chain. Before closing, add a color 2 glass ring to each side of the ring and also two color 1 rings. Close the ring **(d)**.

5. As in step 4, weave a large-thin ring through the third and second adjacent units in the chain. Do not close yet **(e)**.

6. Before closing, weave the thin ring through the color 2 ring from step 4 and add a color 1 glass ring to that same side. Keep the ring open **(f, g)**.

7. Add a color 2 ring on the other side of the ring and finally add a color 1 ring. Close the ring. Each new large-thin ring that is added has to have the glass rings added in this exact way to ensure the color pattern works correctly **(h, i)**.

8. Repeat steps 5–7 for the full length **(j–m)**.

9. Repeat steps 4–8 on the other side of your bracelet, creating a bottom row. It may be helpful to flip the whole bracelet up so that the weaving orientation is the same **(n–q)**.

10. Add a medium ring to every pair of adjacent color 1 glass rings. Close each ring **(r, s)**. The weave is flipped upside down so that you can clearly see the medium rings.

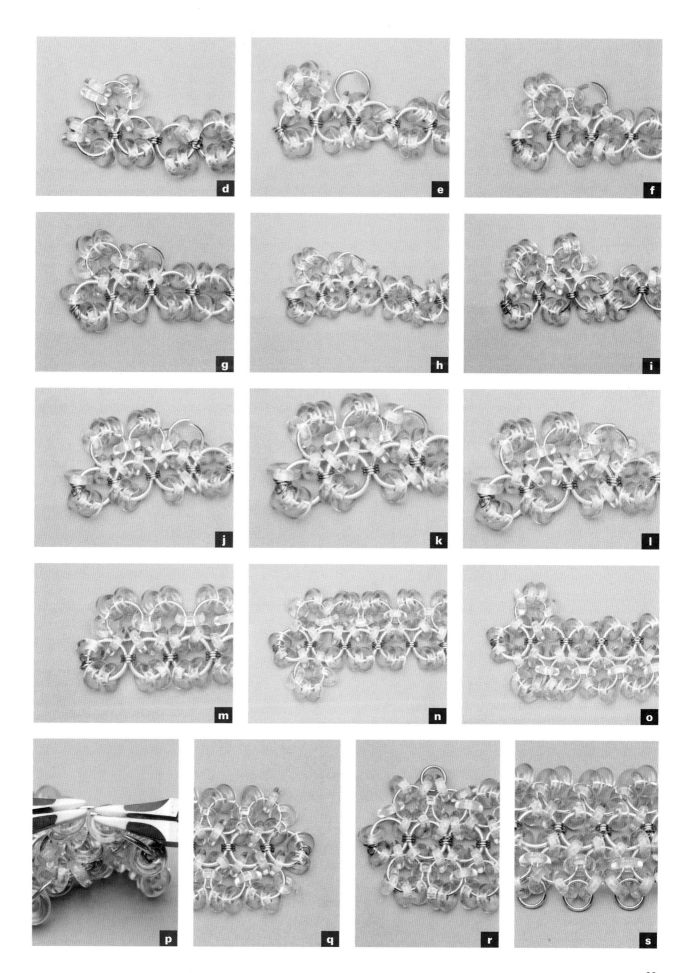

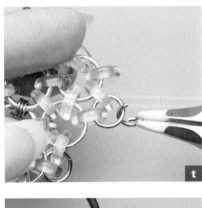

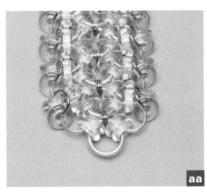

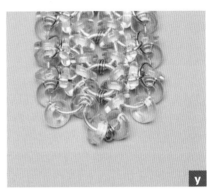

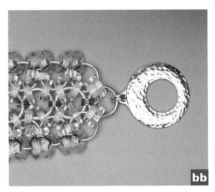

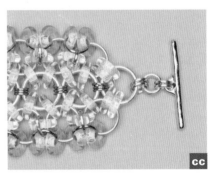

11. Weave a small ring through the medium ring and also bring it down to toward the center of the weave to go through the color 2 glass ring (clear). You have to open the small rings a bit wider than normal in order for it to get through the glass ring. Don't close it yet **(t, u)**.

12. Add a bead and close this ring. It is quite difficult to close this ring because there is very little room to close it. Use the tweezer roundnose pliers, which are helpful here **(v, w)**.

13. Repeat steps 11 and 12 along both edges of the bracelet **(x)**.

14. To bring your piece to a finish, remove one color 1 glass ring from each of the outer rows at both ends of the bracelet. Remove the final two glass rings and tiny rings from the center row at both ends of your bracelet. Keep this ring open **(y, z)**.

15. Weave through the remaining color 2 glass rings with the center large-thick ring. Close the ring **(aa)**.

16. Add the toggle with one or two tiny clasp rings **(bb)**.

17. At the other end of the bracelet, add the toggle bar as shown with tiny and small clasp rings **(cc)**.

space oddity pendant

"Ground control to major Tom." This design reminded me of something exotic that could possibly be found in outer space. It also looks like a beautiful snowflake.

REFERENCE	METAL/TYPE	QTY	RING SIZE	RING GAUGE		AR
				SWG	MM	
large rubber ring	silicone rubber, white	12	3/8 in. (9.5mm)	16	1.6	6.5
rubber ring	silicone rubber, white	12	7/64 in. (2.8mm)	19	1	2.8
large glass ring, color 1	Czech glass, opaque turquoise	4	14mm OD	—	—	2.2
large glass ring, color 2	Czech glass, white opal	2	14mm OD	—	—	2.2
glass ring, color 1	Czech glass, antique blueberry	4	9mm OD	—	—	1.8
glass ring, color 2	Czech glass, white	2	9.5mm OD	—	—	1.5
extra-large ring	aluminum	1	3/4 in. (19.05mm)	14	2	10.8
large-thick ring	aluminum	1	1/4 in. (6.4mm)	16	1.6	4.2
large-thin ring	aluminum	1	1/4 in. (6.4mm)	18	1.2	5.7
medium ring	aluminum	20	3/16 in. (4.8mm)	18	1.2	4.1
tiny ring	aluminum	6	5/32 in. (4mm)	18	1.2	3.6
rhodium-plated swivel lobster claw clasp						

Tools: 2 pairs of large flatnose pliers and 2 pairs of regular flatnose pliers
Length of Time: 2 hours or less

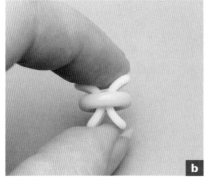

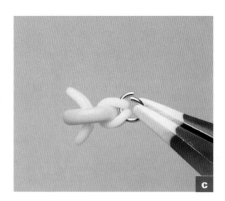

Prep: Close the extra-large ring. Open all of the other rings.

1. Add two rubber rings to each large glass ring **(a, b)**.
2. Fold a rubber ring around the large glass ring and secure it by weaving a medium ring through the loops. Do not close the ring yet **(c)**.

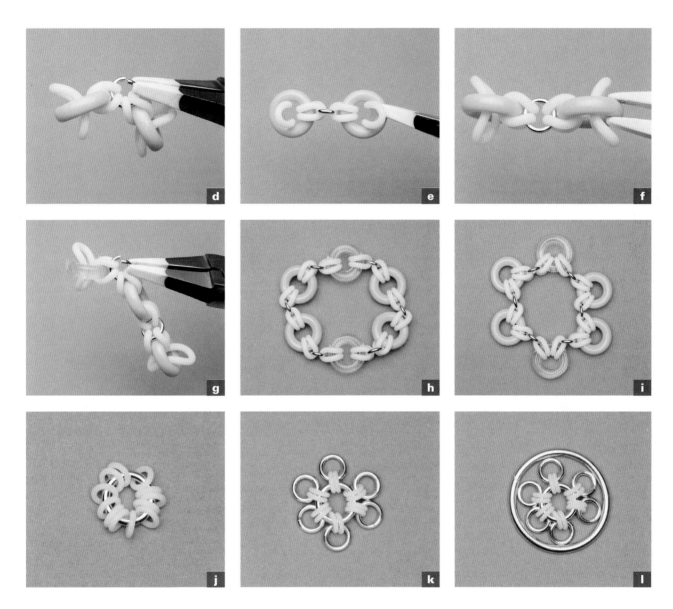

3. Fold a rubber ring from another unit and slide it onto the open medium ring. Now close the ring **(d–f)**.

4. Continue making a chain of folded rubber rings connected by medium rings. Use all of the glass-rubber units from step 1, however as you connect them put two of the same color glass together and then connect the other color glass ring. Connect the final unit to the first unit **(g–h)**.

5. Push the rubber rings together down toward the center and pull the large glass rings out to form points. Set this unit aside **(i)**.

6. Add 12 tiny rubber rings to a large ring. Close the ring **(j)**.

7. To each pair of tiny rubber rings, add a tiny ring. Close each ring **(k)**.

8. Rest the tiny rubber ring unit inside of the extra-large closed ring. Then place the unit completed in step 5 around the extra-large ring **(l, m)**.

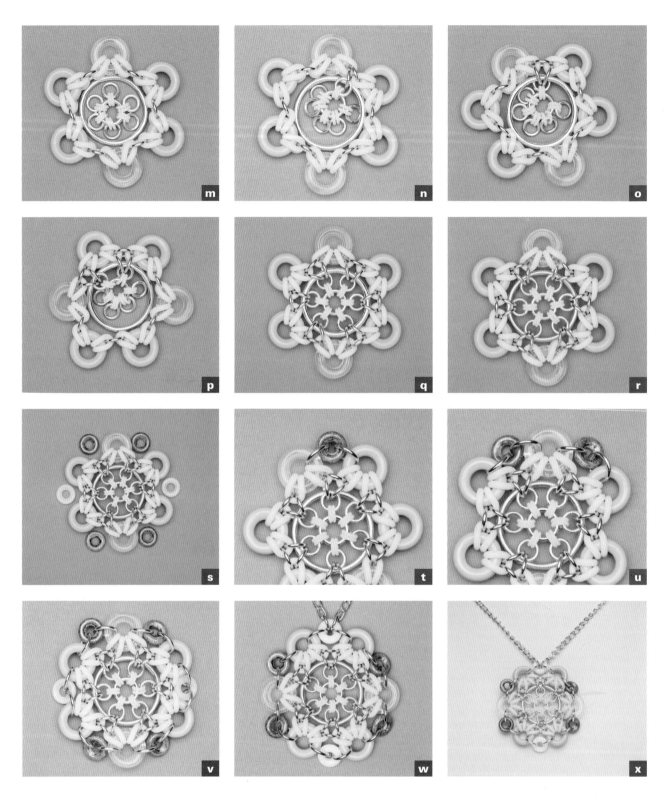

9. Connect the tiny rubber ring unit to the extra-large ring and the large glass-rubber ring unit by weaving a medium ring through the large rubber ring **(n)**.

10. Repeat step 14 all the way around the inside **(o–r)**.

11. Next, we will add small glass rings in between each large glass ring **(s)**.

12. Connect a color 1 small glass ring to two different color large glass rings with large-thin rings **(t)**.

13. Repeat step 12 around the rest of the pendant, paying attention to where each color is place so that the pendant is symmetrical **(u, v)**.

14. As glass rings are sometimes tricky to fit into a pattern well, the white opal rings were too thin and would not sit firmly between the large glass rings. You can switch out any rings that are too thin for thicker small glass rings.

15. Connect to a pre-made chain with medium rings **(w, x)**. Refer to the "Finishing a pre-made chain" section on p. 15.

interstellar pendant

Based on a weave named Hourglass, here comes the glass-accented, star-shaped Interstellar Pendant! This weave only works in stronger metals with more springback, such as stainless steel, bronze, jewelry brass, and aluminum. I do not recommend copper or sterling for this weave, as those metals are quite soft and the rings may pry open over time.

REFERENCE	METAL/TYPE	QTY	RING SIZE	RING GAUGE		AR
				SWG	MM	
steel rings	stainless steel	20–25	21/64 in. (8.3mm)	18	1.2	9.1
bronze rings	bronze	15	21/64 in. (8.3mm)	18	1.2	9.1
medium rings	aluminum	3	13/64 in. (5.2mm)	18	1.2	4.6
large glass ring, color 1	Czech glass, teal	1	14mm OD	—	—	2.2

stainless steel lobster claw clasp

Tools: 2 pairs of flatnose pliers
Length of Time: 2 1/2 hours or less

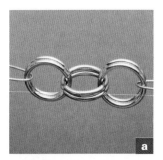

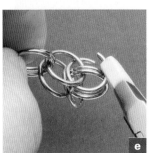

Prep: Close 10 large stainless steel rings. Open all other rings.

1. Create a chain containing three pairs of steel rings **(a)**.
2. While hanging the pairs of rings, weave a bronze ring in between the middle pair of rings. Close the ring. It will rest on one side of the bottom pair of steel rings **(b–d)**.
3. Twist the weave a half-turn and repeat step 2, allowing another bronze ring to rest on the opposite side of the bottom pair of steel rings. It should feel tight to maneuver this ring into position. If you are familiar with Helm weave, you may notice how you are create a modified version of this weave. You may need to tug on this rug to force it to sit directly next to the previous bronze ring. They should not overlap **(e–g)**.
4. Repeat steps 2 and 3 with two bronze rings weaving through the same middle pair of rings. These two bronze rings should rest on the first pair of steel rings. The bronze rings form an "X" shape **(h–k)**.

This unit should be quite firm and the four bronze rings should not move and create an hourglass-like shape. Because this particular ring size can vary slightly from batch to batch, you may need to add a third steel ring on each end to tighten this unit. Pay special attention at this point to the tightness of the unit before adding any additional rings. Decide here if additional steel rings should be added to each end **(l, m)**.

5. Scoop two closed steel rings onto an open steel ring. Weave it through only the doubled (or tripled) "helm" rings on the outside of the "X." Close the ring **(n, o)**.
6. Weave an open steel ring through the back of the hanging pair of steel rings and turn your wrist to bring the open ring up to weave it through the two "helm" rings (the doubled or tripled rings). You are creating an extension that is nearly identical to what you started with in step 1 **(p–r)**.

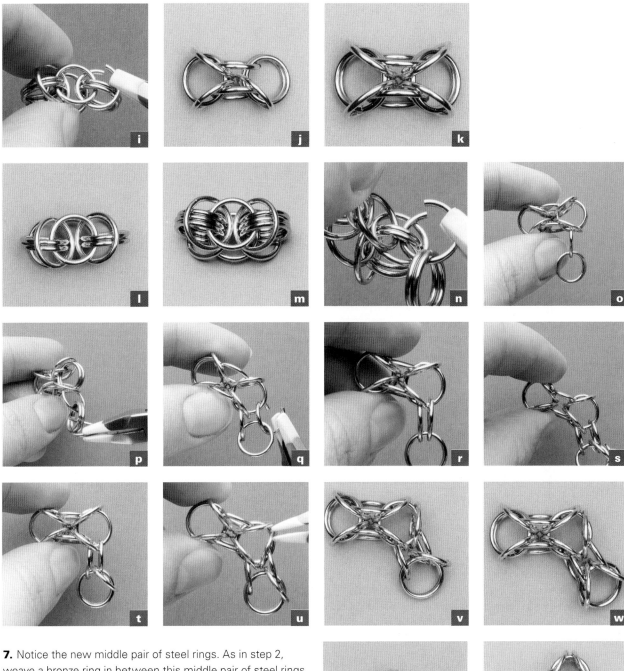

7. Notice the new middle pair of steel rings. As in step 2, weave a bronze ring in between this middle pair of steel rings. Close the ring **(s, t)**.

8. Just above the bronze ring from the previous step, weave a bronze ring through the same middle pair or rings. This ring completes the top half of the "X" shape and slightly touches the bronze ring within the first unit **(u, v)**.

9. You may have been able to guess that we will need to now to complete the entire "X" shape, a.k.a. the Hourglass shape, with one more bronze ring. This is similar to completing step 4 **(w)**.

10. Turn the weave just slightly to see the top point of the star and its two "arms." You will work along the inside of each arm to create shared Hourglass units. The five points of the Interstellar star are formed by shared inner rings of adjacent Hourglass units (the rings that form the "X") **(x)**.

11. Repeat step 6 on the inside of the "arm" completed **(y)**.

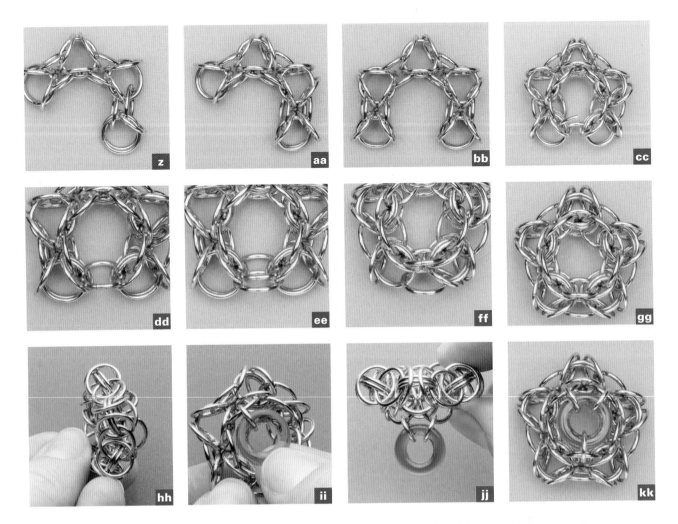

12. Repeat steps 7–10 **(z, aa)**.

13. Continue in a clockwise direction. Repeat steps 12 and 13 to complete another arm with the Hourglass inside. Rotate the weave to form a top point **(bb)**.

14. To join the two arms together, start by weaving a steel ring through the Helm rings on the inside of one of the arms. Before closing, also weave it through the Helm (doubled or tripled) rings on the inside of the final arm. Close the ring **(cc, dd)**.

15. Add a steel ring to the same Helm rings on each arm, but this time, weave it on the outside of the bronze rings. You have created the center pair of rings as in previous steps **(ee)**.

16. Complete the hourglass shape by adding in two bronze rings as in previous steps **(ff, gg)**. The unit should be quite firm and bow out or curve a bit **(hh)**.

17. Weave a medium (aluminum) ring around a large glass ring and also around the steel ring directly below the center of an Hourglass unit. Close the ring **(ii)**.

18. Add a second medium ring through the glass and around the steel ring directly below the center of the adjacent Hourglass unit **(jj)**.

19. Add a final medium ring through the glass and around the ring attached to the center of the bottom Hourglass unit. This ring is difficult to weave in place and you may need to gently pull the glass toward the bottom unit with the open medium rings **(kk)**. You can run a thin chain through the back of the top point and finish the chain ends.

glossary

Alloy: Refers to a metal made by combining two or more metallic elements. For example, bronze is an alloy of copper and tin.

American Wire Gauge (AWG): A measurement system for used for most non-ferrous metals, which would include precious metals such as sterling and niobium. Also known as Brown & Sharpe. NOTE: Although aluminum, brass, bronze and copper are considered non-ferrous the suppliers I use for these rings use the Standard Wire Gauge (SWG) system for measuring these rings. All rings in this book are measured by SWG standards.

Anodized: The electrical process that metal has gone through to give it color. Anodized aluminum (AA) goes through a slightly different anodizing process than anodized niobium & titanium. The aluminum is electrically treated to become porous and then dyed to obtain its color. It may also receive a clear coat for shine and to seal in the color. The color can be scratched by pliers or by other rough surfaces. It also fades over time due to sunlight exposure, contact with acidic skin and normal wear.

Aspect Ratio (AR): The ratio used to describe the relationship between the inner diameter (ID) and the wire diameter (WD). Use one consistent unit of measurement (either millimeters or decimal inches) to calculate AR by using this formula: AR = ID ÷ WD.

Base Metal: Generally used to describe many metals that are not considered precious metals. For the purposes of this book, base metals refer to aluminum, copper, jewelry brass, bronze and steel.

Bright Aluminum (BA): A specific alloy of aluminum that has a very bright silver appearance, and resists oxidation. Bright aluminum is cleaner and shinier and produces far less black "rub off" than regular aluminum. It has quite a bit of springback and takes practice to close jump rings well. This is not a very durable metal in 20 gauge and thinner.

Chain Mail: Chain mail can be spelled a variety of ways including, chainmaille and chainmail. Also affectionately referred to simply as "maille," which is French for "mesh." It traditionally is defined as flexible armor of interlinked metal rings. It is still used to make armor, and has also morphed in various other forms including fashion, jewelry, and more.

Coiling (wire): The process in which wire is wrapped around a mandrel in one direction and each loop is pushed tightly against each other. The coil is then pulled off of the mandrel and cut and the result is jump rings.

Hairline Opening: When the jump ring has not been closed completely and you can see a thin opening through the closure. These can be fixed by re-opening the ring and creating more overlap before bringing it to a close.

Inner Diameter (ID): The inside of a jump ring. The measurement does not include the wire diameter (or gauge). Measurements are given a variety of different ways including inches, millimeters and fractional inches. The inner diameter of a jump ring is affected by springback, wire diameter, and the type of metal used during the coiling process. When making chainmaille, the inner diameter is the most helpful measurement compared to the outer diameter (OD).

Jump Rings: The basic ring shape created during the coiling and cutting process. Jump rings are always just a little bit "open" and need to be closed completely to keep the chain mail item stable.

Kerf: The width of the cut made by the saw when jump rings are cut from the coil. Thinner kerfs mean the jump rings are more circular and easier to close.

Mandrel: The metal rod that the wire is coiled around to make jump rings. Suppliers may sell their rings in inch increments or millimeter increments, which indicates what type of mandrel was used.

Machine Cut: Rings that are cut by a machine after they are coiled are called machine-cut. These differ from saw-cut because they have a slight divit or triangle shaped cut and are not as smooth in appearance. A machine cut ring will not appear seamless when closed. You will see and feel the closure. None of the rings used in this book are machine cut.

Non-Ferrous Metal: Metals that do not contain iron are non-ferrous. Metals that are non-ferrous are aluminum, copper, nickel, tin, titanium, bronze, brass, sterling, gold, niobium. Stainless steel and iron are ferrous metals and have superior resistance to corrosion.

Offset: I use this word to refer to jump rings that are not fully closed yet, where one side of the ring does not fully meet flush with the other end. These offset rings can be fixed by holding one side of the jump ring steady and gently pushing or pulling the other side until the ends are perfectly flush.

Outer Diameter (OD): The outside of a jump ring. The measurement does include the wire diameter (or gauge). Measurements are given a variety of different ways including inches, millimeters and fractional inches. The outer diameter of a jump ring is affected by springback, wire diameter, and the type of metal used during the coiling process. Note that bead manufacturers and bead suppliers many times use only outer diameters for the listed measurements.

Overbite: I use this term to refer to a jump ring that has been closed improperly where one side of the ring is higher than the other side and the ends are not perfectly flush. Rings with an overbite can sometimes be fixed by, carefully re-opening the ring, and then slightly pulling up on the side that is too low as you close the ring.

Overlap: When closing the ring, each side of the ring has to slightly overlap each other to eliminate the kerf and a possible hairline opening. Some rings with more springback require more overlapping than others.

Oxidize (Oxidation): Oxidize is defined as "to combine with oxygen". In reference to chainmaille rings that oxidize, it means that they have changed in hue due to the exposure to air. This is also called tarnish or a patina. Metals that contain copper oxidize (tarnish) to a darker color over time with normal wear.

Precious Metal: Generally refers to a metal that is not considered a base metal (as defined above). Precious metals include sterling, niobium, platinum, gold, and palladium.

Pringled: A common reference for rings that have been closed improperly so the end result is a saddle-shaped or pringled (like the potato chip) ring. These rings can sometimes be fixed by re-opening them and gently pushing each side of the ring in the opposite direction of the pringle as it is being closed.

Raw Rings: Rings that have not been opened or closed yet.

Saw-Cut: Rings that are cut with a thin rotating saw blade. These rings have a seamless closure and are preferred to machine-cut for fine jewelry. When saw-cut rings are closed properly, you can barely see or feel the closure.

Speed Weaving: Cutting down the steps it takes to complete a weave by combining steps or finding an easier method is referred to as speed weaving. There are various speed weaving techniques, such as adding in extra rings as others are being woven so that they are ready for you in a following step.

Spring Back: The amount of resistance the wire gives after it is coiled. It springs back and relaxes from the shape into which it is being wound. Aluminum, bronze and steel have a harder temper and have far more spring back than copper and brass, which are considered to be softer metals.

Standard Wire Gauge (SWG): A measurement system also know as Imperial Wire Gauge, used for most ferrous metals, which would include stainless steel. All rings used in this book are measured by SWG standards, including the non-ferrous metals.

Tarnish: See "oxidize."

Temper: The hardness or softness of wire. Certain metals have a harder temper than others. There are various tempers of wire, including, dead soft, soft, half-hard, and full-hard.

Tumbling: A method of cleaning and polishing jump rings, finished jewelry and more. For the purposes of this book, rotary wet-media tumbling is discussed in detail. Vibratory dry tumbling is used to highly polish and deburr various materials and is not a method I use for cleaning. This is a similar process to rock tumbling.

Weave: The unique pattern created by the linking of rings. There are thousands of known chainmaille weaves and variations of original weaves.

Wire Diameter (WD): The measured thickness of the wire for jump rings. The wire gauge number and its millimeter SWG measurement are given for each jump ring within each project.

Wire Gauge (g or ga): An assigned number used to describe the thickness of a wire. The smaller the number, the thicker the wire is. 12 gauge wire is thicker than 24 gauge. Wire gauges are inconsistent depending on the measurement system used (AWG vs. SWG). Also different sources may list a single wire gauge number with slightly different actual measurements. Commonly used SWG jump ring wire gauges are 22, 20, 18, 16, 14 and 12. AWG gauges have both even and odd numbers such as the common ones : 13, 14, 15, 16, 17, 18, 19, 20.

Work Hardened: The process in which a metal is strengthened. The process may include hammering, opening and closing a jump ring, bending, twisting and turning it, etc. Only some metal jump rings can be work-hardened in a beneficial way such as copper, enameled copper, brass, and bronze. Other jump ring metals that are work-hardened will become brittle and break with too much manipulation including, aluminum, anodized aluminum, and even stainless steel.

ACKNOWLEDGMENTS

Adam Wisniewski is my brother and one of the most driven people I know. He's always been my champion and I've learned how to seek what I want in life by watching his example. Jose Sanchez, my husband, offered his unwavering support, even when it meant putting everything else on hold; I'm also so thankful for Jose's help with the many, many hours of photographing each project.

Thank you to the following: My parents, for their support and for teaching me to work hard for everything that I want to accomplish in life. Vanessa Walilko, for giving me a very strong push to write this book; she's an amazing artist and I'm happy to call her my friend. Over the past 11 years, my students have taught me so much and I've gained so much experience and inspiration from their enthusiasm. To Blue Buddha Boutique for providing many of the needed rings for the projects and also for the many years of teaching experience. To Rebeca Mojica for providing advice and answering my many questions about writing a chain mail book. To Mhai O Mhai Beads and Hyperlynks for providing the wonderful kits for the book and perfecting the supplies to make sure the readers enjoy the full experience! To Wubbers, Lindstrom, and Tronex for accepting my request and providing expert tools to use for the book.

To Pam at Lill Street Art Center, for allowing me to gain so much teaching experience; the various local bead stores where I've added even more teaching experience; the chainmaille, (aka chain maille, chain mail) community via all the suppliers, forums, and groups—you all keep me on my toes and inspire me daily; the entire team at Kalmbach Publishing, especially Erica, for publishing my first book and answering hours of questions; my furry babies, Lloyd, Nacho, Sesame, and Gaby for providing the much-needed stress relief that they are experts at providing; Zoe Keating, Meshell NdegeOcello, and David Bowie for creating the most beautiful music to make the process feel just a bit smoother.

ABOUT THE AUTHOR

Kat Wisniewski is an inventive and dedicated pioneer in the craft of chain mail. In 2003, she learned the craft by finding chain mail weave photos online and printing them larger in order to decipher how the rings interacted. She bought various rings from craft stores, opened them with her fingers and terrible pliers and then some how figured out how to push the rings into the proper positions to match the photos. It took a few months before she realized there were online tutorials and ring suppliers. She was so enthusiastic about the craft, that she started teaching chain mail within just a few months of learning it.

Kat has won various awards for her work, and is well known for her 15 chain mail tutorials, including her famous Glass Caterpillar Bracelet pattern. She has published many tutorials with Blue Buddha Boutique, *Wirework*, and *Step-by-Step Wire Jewelry* magazines. Kat has also ghost-written 42 of Blue Buddha Boutique's tutorials.Kat has taught at many locations in the Chicagoland area and currently continues to teach at Lill Street Art Center and Blue Buddha Boutique. You can also find Kat's work via her jewelry company, Elemental Art Jewelry and at various fine art shows in the Chicagoland area. Please visit the book's website, www.newconnectionsbook.com, for more details on the projects, tools, bonus info, and more!